Kawaii CROSS STITCH Patterns

"Dedicated to all who add
a little cuteness and playfulness
to this world
with the work of their hands."

Sakura Mai

Table of contents

Animals 1

Panda in a coffee cup 1
Bear loves honey 2
Happy bunny 3
Cat holding a cupcake 4
Unicorn and a cat in cups 5
Hamster 6
Lovely elephant holding a flower 7
Fox in the forest 8
Cat with the food 9
Cat in the gym 10
Lovely snake 11
Baby dinosaur holding a heart 12
Koala 13
Cat and dog on a yellow duck 14
Dancing bear 15
A baby bear in the garden 16
Lion 17

Creatures (real and fantasy) 18

Unicorn on a pink flamingo 18
Fairy with a magic wand 19
Unicorn holding a flower 20
Mermaid princess with a star 21
Tooth Fairy 22
Mermaid with a heart 23
Mermaid princess with a cup 24
Little girl holding a baby unicorn 25
Pilot unicorn fly on an airplane 26
Unicorn sleeping on a cloud 27
Princess with a unicorn whale 28
Caticorn on a cloud 29
Unicorn girl holding a strawberry cupcake 30
Pegasus flying on pastel sky 31
Princess with a pony 32
Unicorn with donuts 33
Unicorn eating a strawberry ice cream 34
Unicorn on sweet cherry and strawberry cake . . 35
Pony wearing Santa hat 36

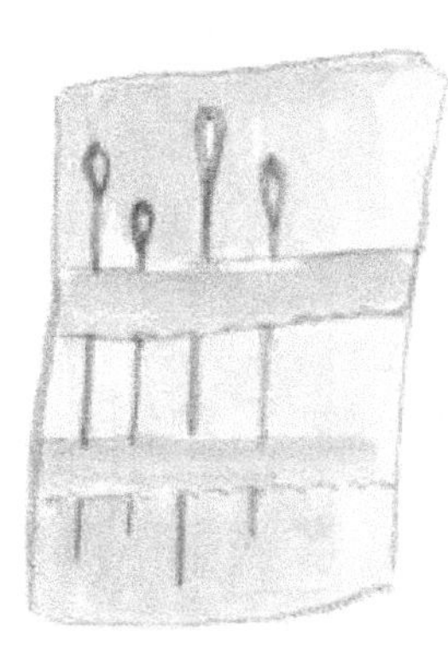

Unicorn eating a yummy donut 37
Unicorn on a cotton candy 38
Caticorn fish holding a star 39
Caticorn fish holding a balloon 40
Unicorn on the moon 41
Unicorn dreaming on an ice cream 42
Unicorn's birthday cake 43
Sleepy unicorn 44
Kids 45
Baby with a yellow duck 46
Baby girl 47
Baby boy 48
Gobelin eating meat 49

Nature 50
Gasteria succulent plant 50
Mom and baby cactus 51
Rainbow and clouds 52
Flying rainbow cloud 53
Rainbow love heart 54
Mother earth 55
Smiley flower 56

Christmas .57
Unicorn climbing the Christmas tree 57
Girl and unicorn in a Christmas stocking .58
Reindeer sitting on a Christmas gift 59
Unicorn with Christmas lights 60
Santa Claus girl 61
Girl flying with a reindeer balloon 62
Lovely unicorn in a cup 63
Snowman 64
Bear holding a Christmas tree 65
Tigger at Christmas 66
Girl wearing a Christmas tree costume . .67

Valentine (Love and gifts) 68
Magician girl with a heart wand 68
Valentine gnome 69
Cupid with heart arrows 70

Happy unicorn holding a heart balloon . . .71
Happy unicorn with the gifts 72
Valentine bunnies 73
Love in the air 74
Cute toilet friends 75
Game console gift 76

Halloween .77
Dracula cat 77
Ghost with a cupcake and candies 78
Cat with a magic pot cauldron 79
Witch girl 80
Funny trick or treat girl 81
Floral unicorn 82
Halloween party girl 83
Girl holding a pumpkin bucket 84
Witch with a big pumpkin 85
Zombie .86
Witch on a broom 87

Drinks and food 88
Fast food 88
Taco 89
Bread and omelet 90
Ramen 91
Avocado in love 92
Burger 93
Fried chicken bucket 94
Sweet macarons with jam 95
Pizza slice 96
Ice cream bar 97
Sushi 98
Rice bowl 99
Cherry Ice cream 100
Coffee with the cookie 101
Strawberry milk 102
Matcha tea 103
Chips 104

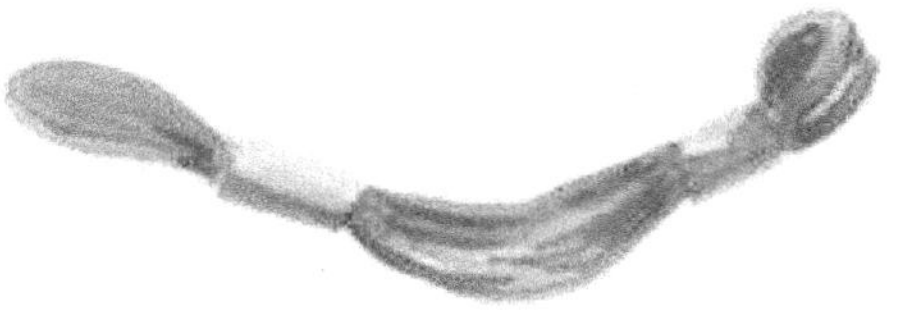
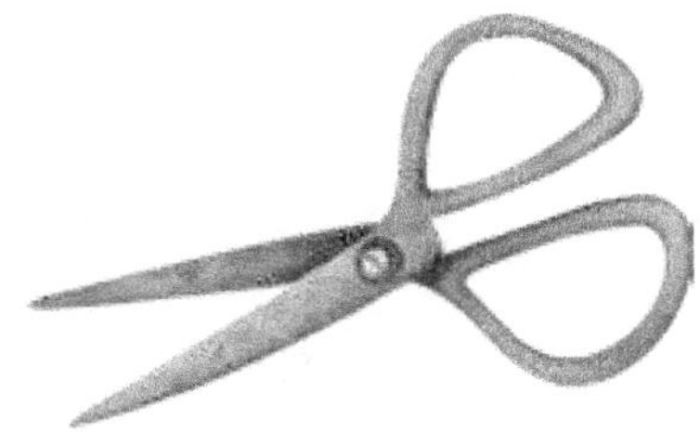

General instructions

Before you start:

Welcome to the world of cross stitch!
This book contains more than 101 one-of-a-kind cross stitch motifs, plenty of cute designs to please everyone like animals, unicorns, food, princesses, fantasy creatures…and more, all made up of full colors with symbols, a preview of the original small artwork beside so you can see what it will look like and color key table for DMC floss.

Fabric

Counted cross-stitch is worked on even-weave fabrics. These fabrics are manufactured specifically for counted-thread embroidery and are woven with the same number of vertical as horizontal threads per inch. The number of threads per inch determines the size of a finished design.

Aida fabric is fantastic for cross stitch as it is an even-weave, it's also a favorite of beginning stitchers because its weave forms distinctive squares in fabric, which makes placing stitches easily and allows you to create straight lines while you stitch, Aida is measured by "count", 14 count Aida has 14 squares per inch, 18 count has 18 squares per inch = the more squares per inch, the smaller the stitches and overall pattern will be.

Number of strands

The number of strands used varies depending on the fabric. Generally, the rule to follow for cross-stitching is three strands in Aida 11, two strands on Aida 14, one or two strands on Aida 18 (depending on the desired thickness of stitches), and one strand on Hardanger 22.
For backstitching, use one strand on all fabrics.

Preparing the fabric

Cut the fabric at least 3 inches larger on each side than the finished design size to ensure enough space for the desired assembly. To prevent fraying, whipstitch, machine-zigzag, or apply a masking tape along the raw edges.

Cleaning the finished design

When you are finished, you can give your fabric a gentle hand wash in cold water and mild soap. Rinse well and roll in a towel to remove excess water. Don't wring, just place it face down on a dry towel and iron on a warm setting until the fabric is dry.

Cross stitch

• Danish method

Consist of doing one half of the stitch in one direction, then coming back to do the other half of the stitch, stitches are done in a row or, if necessary, one at a time in an area.

This method is ideal for working in big blocks of color, as you can go in one direction then back ending up at the beginning of the next row or column. This method uses less treads and leaves the back of your work neat.

Steps:

1. Insert needle up between interlacing threads at A.
2. Go down at B. the opening diagonally across from A.
3. Come up at C and go down at D, etc.
4. To complete the top stitches creating an "X" come up at E and go down at B, come up at C and go down at F, etc. All top stitches should be in the same direction.

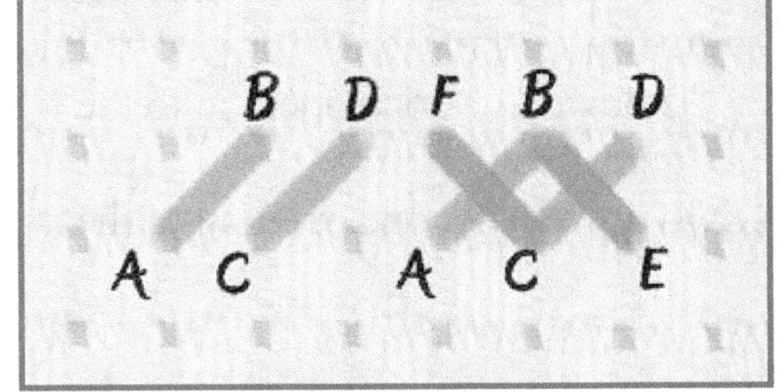

• English method

Consist of completing each cross at once, it's often the easier method to use when handling some randomly scattered stitches of one color across your pattern.

Steps:
1. Insert needle up between interlacing threads at A.
2. Go down at B. the opening diagonally across from A.
3. Come up at C and go down at D to complete a full "X".
4. To continue the second "X" come up at E and go down at D, come up at B and go down at F, etc...

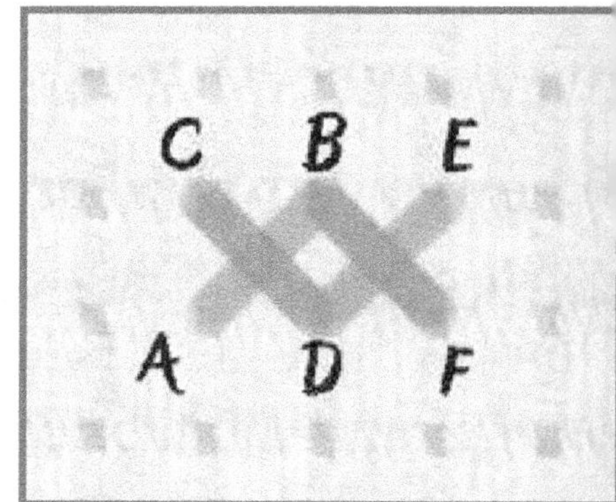

There is no right or wrong way to do cross stitch and It's all about experimenting with both methods, the more you stitch, the more you will discover your own rhythm and see which one works best for you most of the time.

Backstitch

Back stitching is usually used for an intricate and detailed design. Though it is not required by the patterns of this book, you can still add it when you feel it's needed.

Steps:
1. Insert needle up between interlacing threads at A.
2. Go down at B. one opening to the right.
3. Come up at C.
4. Go down at A. one opening to the right.

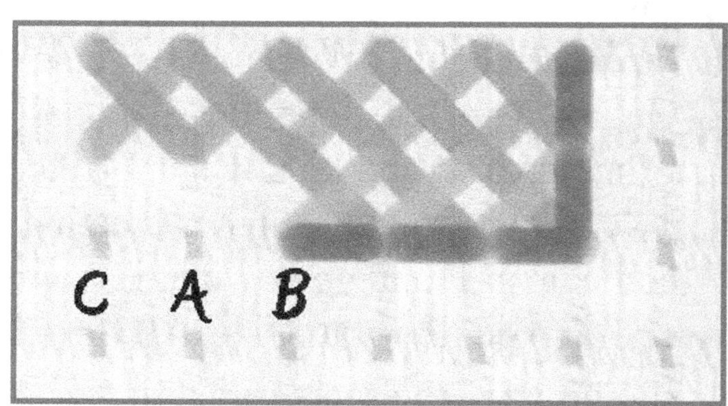

How to adjust the patterns to be bigger or smaller?

The simplest method is to use the pattern as is, but you need to alter the size or count number of your Aida cloth!

If you would like your design to be larger, use a smaller count, such as 6, 8, or 11 count Aida cloth, which has larger squares (fewer squares per inch) and can make your finished design larger. This method will work if you'd prefer to reduce your pattern size too, just use less count Aida like 18 or 24, and your finished design will come out smaller.

How to figure out how much bigger (or smaller) it will be?

The general rule is simple! Here's the math:

Stitch count of design / Aida cloth count = finished size in inches

Note that you will have to make 2 calculations: 1 for the length and 1 for the width.

Example: We have 28 squares in the width and let's say we decide to use 14 squares of Aida fabric :

28 stitches / 14 count Aida = 2 inch

These are the dimensions rule for all the patterns in this book:
Final fabric dimensions for 7 squares per inch fabric: 17.14x17.14 inches
Final fabric dimensions for 10 squares per inch fabric: 12.00x12.00 inches
Final fabric dimensions for 11 squares per inch fabric: 10.9x10.91 inches
Final fabric dimensions for 12 squares per inch fabric: 10.00x10.00 inches
Final fabric dimensions for 14 squares per inch fabric: 8.57x8.57 inches
Final fabric dimensions for 16 squares per inch fabric: 750x750 inches
Final fabric dimensions for 18 squares per inch fabric: 6.67x6.67 inches
Final fabric dimensions for 20 squares per inch fabric: 6.00x6.00 inches
Final fabric dimensions for 22 squares per inch fabric: 5.45x5.45 inches
Final fabric dimensions for 24 squares per inch fabric: 5.00x5.00 inches
Final fabric dimensions for 25 squares per inch fabric: 4.80x4.80 inches
Final fabric dimensions for 28 squares per inch fabric: 4.29x4.29 inches

Tips

- Your thread count and the amount of strands you use change your pattern's outcome, I suggest you to use three strands instead of two if you are looking for more coverage.
- Use beads, sequins, charms, buttons, and other embellishments to change the overall style of a finished piece. Match elements to the style you are going for, and take care not to overdo it. Only one of these elements is usually best. These elements can also be a good filler for negative space on your fabric background.
- You can combine a multiple designs to create your own piece of art!

Panda in a coffee cup

		Count	Code	Name
★		906	310	Black
⊡		748	413	Pewter Gray Dark
▲		693	603	Cranberry
⊞		500	964	Sea Green Light
⌶		304	3855	Autumn Gold Lt
≣		564	415	Pearl Gray
⌘		2536	828	Sky Blue Vy Lt
◡		1361	White	White

Bear loves honey

		Count	Code	Name
★	■	585	310	Black
⊡		44	666	Bright Red
▲		370	3045	Yellow Beige Dk
⊞		190	725	Topaz Med Lt
≡		1657	3864	Mocha Beige Light
⌣		209	White	White

Happy bunny

		Count	Code	Name
★	■	866	310	Black
⊞		442	725	Topaz Med Lt
▲		106	341	Blue Violet Light
≣		20	472	Avocado Grn U Lt
◆		738	3609	Plum Ultra Light
⊠		202	828	Sky Blue Vy Lt
⌘		594	3713	Salmon Very Light
∪		2027	White	White

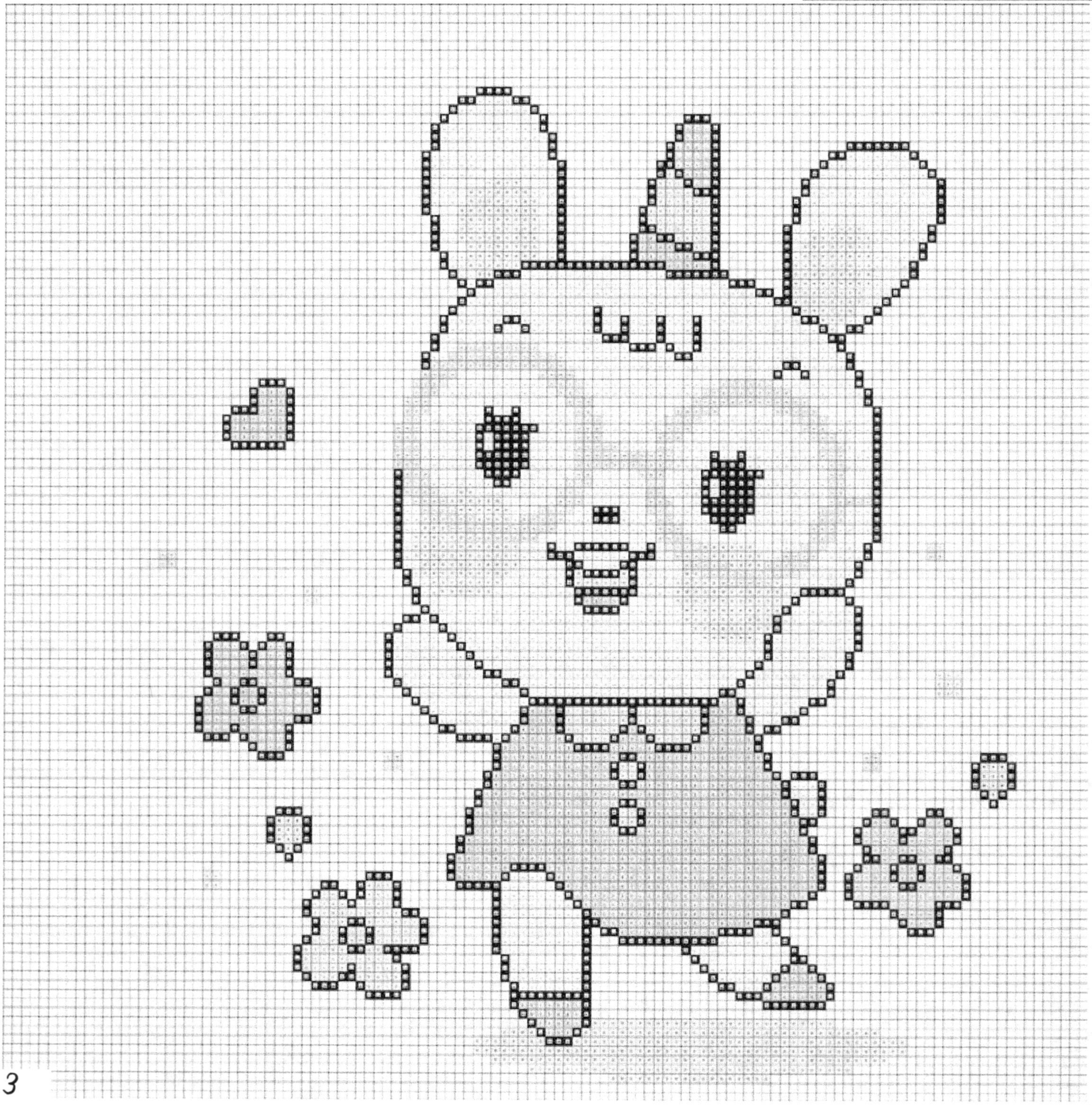

3

Cat holding a cupcake

		Count	Code	Name
★		146	791	Cornflower Blue V D
		2	702	Kelly Green
▲		21	351	Coral
		1009	156	Blue Violet Med Lt
		376	738	Tan Very Light
⊗		1861	157	Cornflower Blue Vy Lt
		97	3326	Rose Light
		182	963	Dusty Rose Ult Vy Lt
+		63	3078	Golden Yellow Vy Lt
		374	White	White

Unicorn and a cat in cups

		Count	Code	Name
★		1052	310	Black
⊡		32	3731	Dusty Rose Very Dark
⊞		539	209	Lavender Dark
⌘		351	155	Blue Violet Med Dark
◆		403	598	Turquoise Light
Ǝ		1895	3608	Plum Very Light
⊼		39	605	Cranberry Very Light
☰		615	3770	Tawny Vy Light
⌣		1115	White	White

Hamster

	Count	Code	Name
★	973	310	Black
+	110	725	Topaz Med Lt
▲	124	340	Blue Violet Medium
◆	386	352	Coral Light
▶	533	778	Antique Mauve Vy Lt
▷	3435	828	Sky Blue Vy Lt
▼	482	3713	Salmon Very Light
▽	70	White	White

lovely elephant holding a flower

		Count	Code	Name
★		702	803	Baby Blue Ult Vy Dk
□		142	3705	Melon Dark
▲		25	744	Yellow Pale
+		2749	828	Sky Blue Vy Lt
≡		2144	963	Dusty Rose Ult Vy Lt
◡		28	White	White

Fox in the forest

	Count	Code	Name
★	722	801	Coffee Brown Dk
▯	23	912	Emerald Green Lt
▲	13	666	Bright Red
⊞	900	3830	Terra Cotta
⊠	634	3863	Mocha Beige Med
▤	1190	608	Burnt Orange Bright
⊘	54	725	Topaz Med Lt
⌘	76	605	Cranberry Very Light
⌣	668	3770	Tawny Vy Light

Cat with the food

		Count	Code	Name
★		1457	3371	Black Brown
⊡		16	561	Celadon Green VD
▲		128	433	Brown Med
⊞		269	321	Red
⊠		95	169	Pewter Light
▤		182	437	Tan Light
⌘		301	3326	Rose Light
⊗		1011	822	Beige Gray Light
⌣		3992	White	White

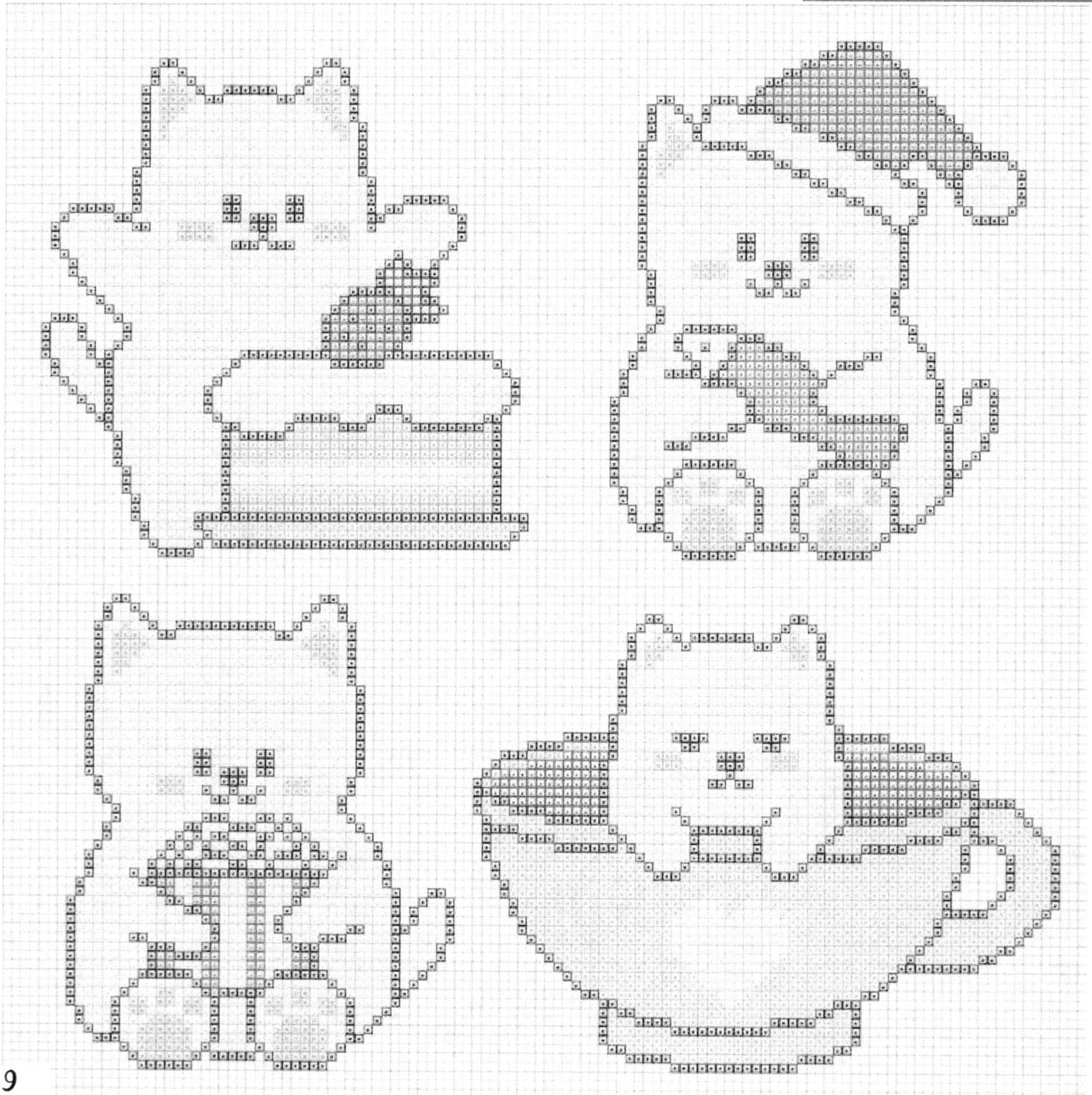

Cat in the gym

		Count	Code	Name
★		1187	3371	Black Brown
□		78	321	Red
▲		593	169	Pewter Light
⊞		109	3326	Rose Light
⊻		12	3325	Baby Blue Light
☰		516	3072	Beaver Gray Vy Lt
⌣		3975	White	White

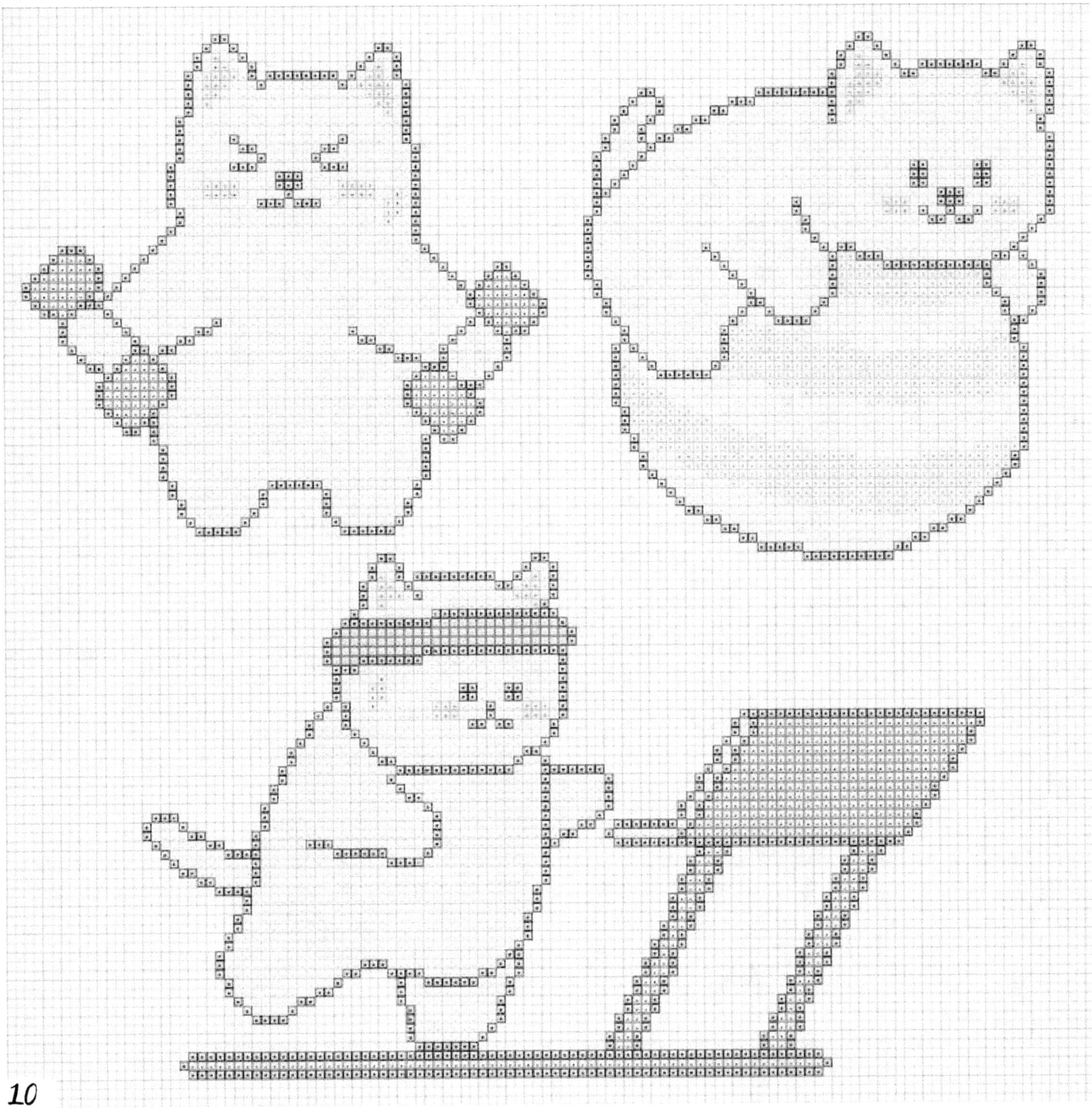

lovely snake

		Count	Code	Name
★		745	801	Coffee Brown Dk
□		1302	987	Forest Green Dk
▲		7	321	Red
≣		2263	703	Chartreuse
╋		172	3805	Cyclamen Pink
✗		613	3819	Moss Green Lt
◡		16	White	White

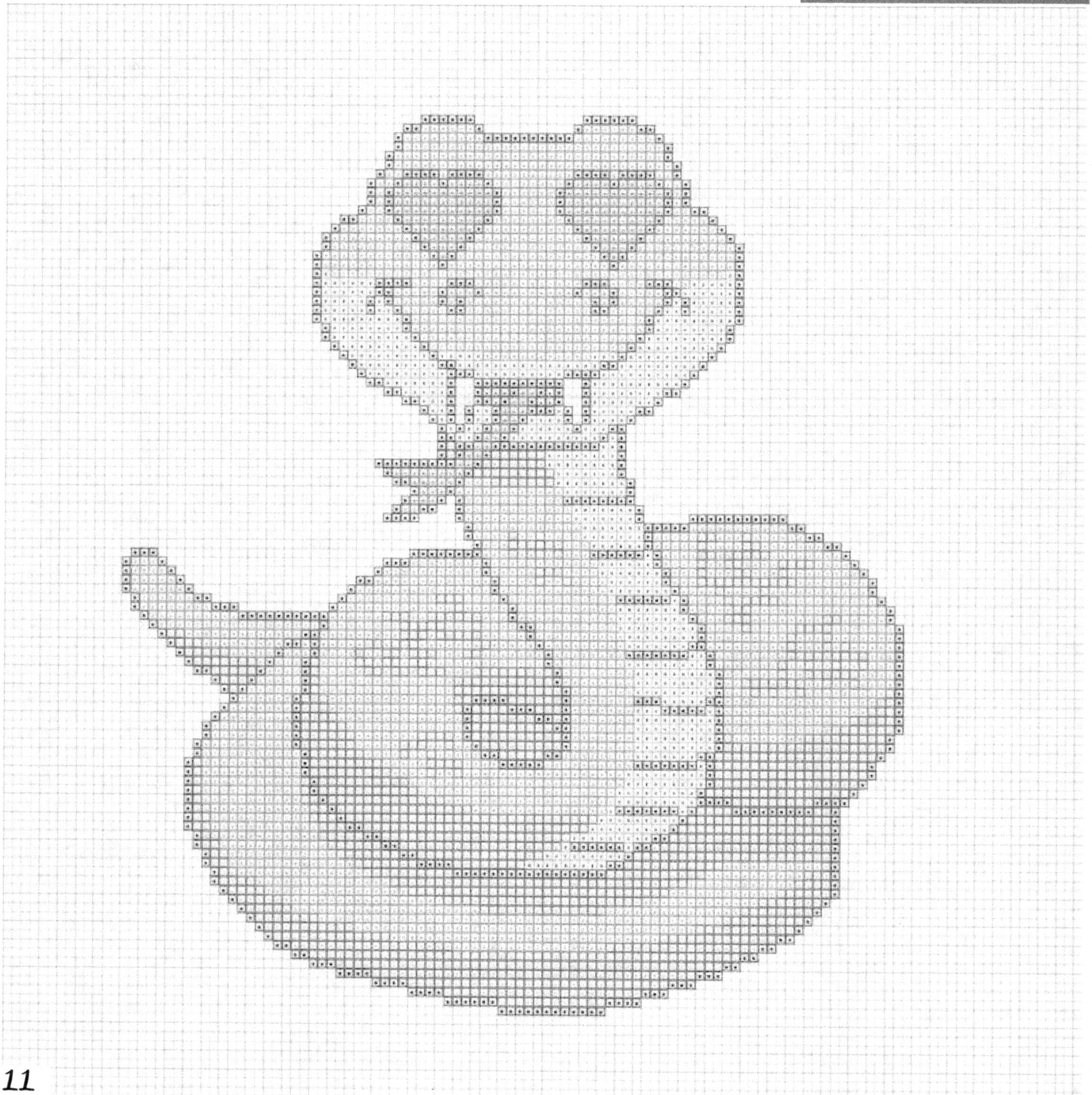

Baby dinosaur holding a heart

		Count	Code	Name
★		91	909	Emerald Green Vy Dk
⊡		633	943	Green Bright Md
▲		2179	993	Aquamarine Vy Lt
⊠		246	828	Sky Blue Vy Lt
+		660	3708	Melon Light
≡		277	928	Gray Green Vy Lt
∪		42	White	White

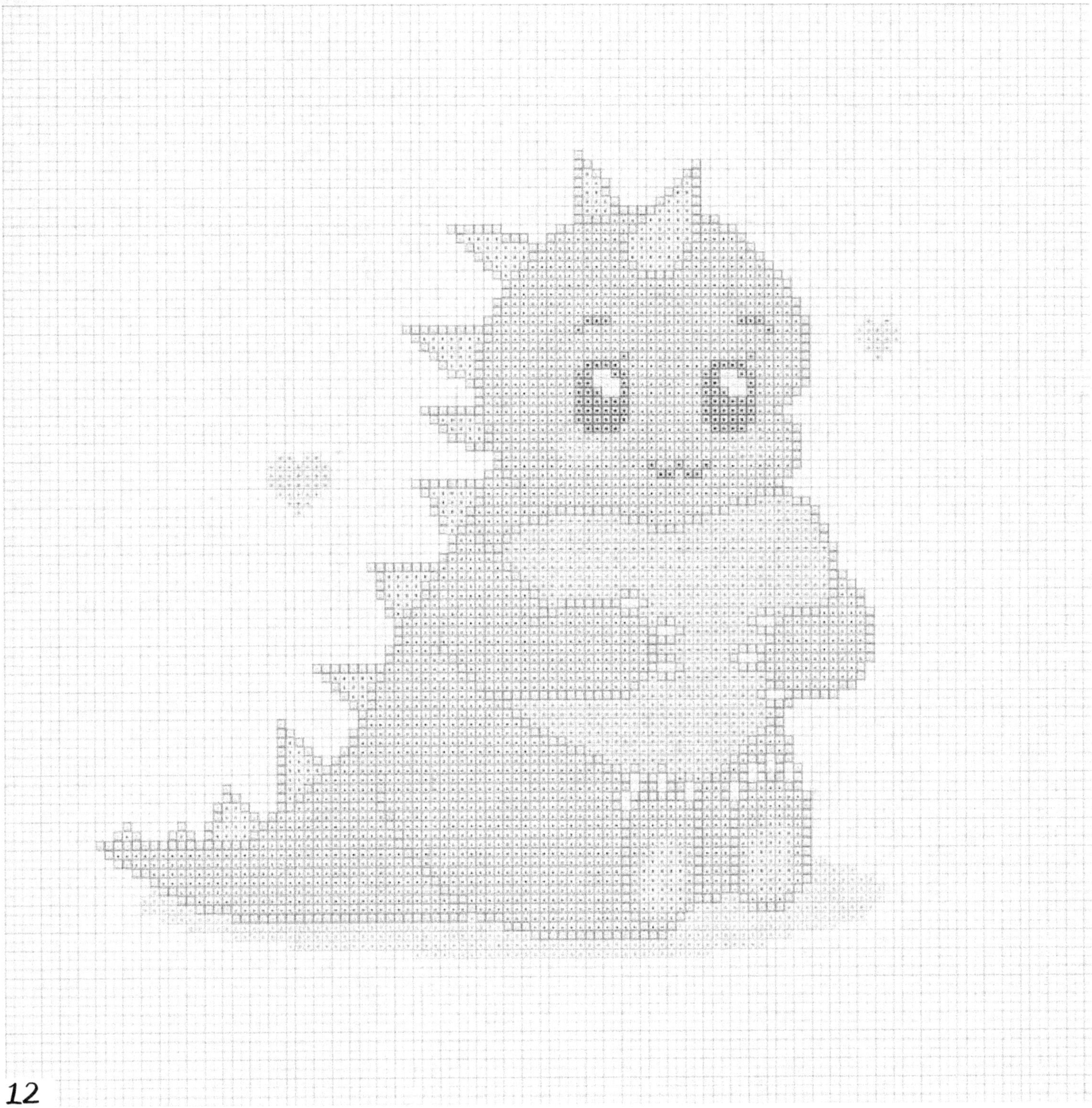

Koala

		Count	Code	Name
★	■	647	823	Navy Blue Dark
☐	▨	20	666	Bright Red
▲	☐	2499	159	Blue Gray Light
+	☐	1168	762	Pearl Gray Vy Lt

Cat and dog on a yellow duck

		Count	Code	Name
★	■	819	310	Black
⊡		9	3350	Dusty Rose Ultra Dark
▲		232	646	Beaver Gray Dk
+		145	3853	Autumn Gold Dk
⊠		1163	3864	Mocha Beige Light
⌘		58	738	Tan Very Light
◆		1832	744	Yellow Pale
≡		153	3841	Baby Blue Pale
⌣		775	White	White

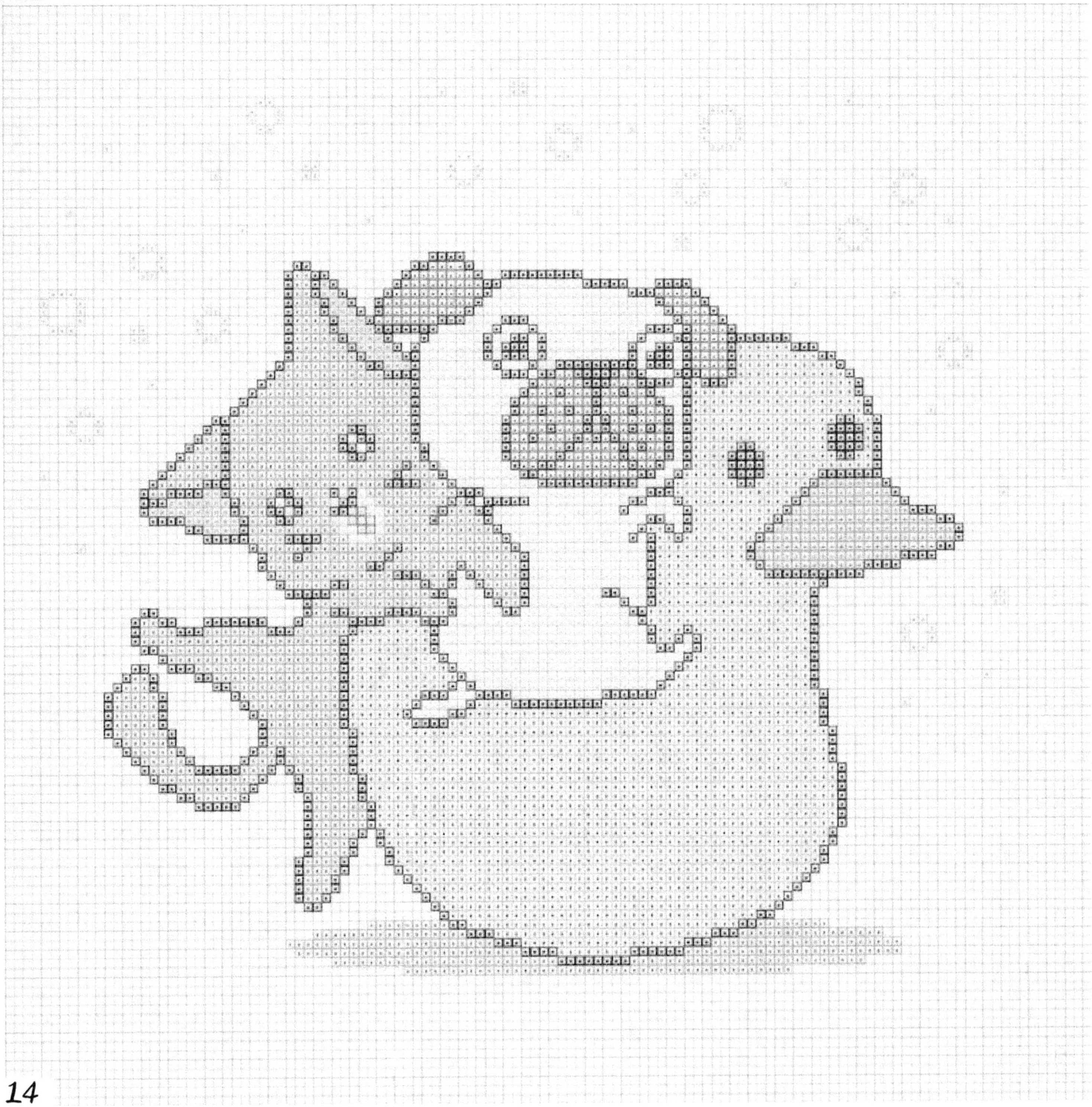

Dancing bear

		Count	Code	Name
★		398	413	Pewter Gray Dark
⊡		11	3843	Electric Blue
▲		44	334	Baby Blue Medium
☰		14	3712	Salmon Medium
┼		224	927	Gray Green Light
⊠		39	3716	Dusty Rose Med Vy Lt
⌘		1491	928	Gray Green Vy Lt
⌣		260	White	White

A baby bear in the garden

		Count	Code	Name
★		1062	3830	Terra Cotta
▫		1801	913	Nile Green Med
▲		225	436	Tan
+		2797	722	Orange Spice Light
≣		293	368	Pistachio Green Lt
✕		107	3806	Cyclamen Pink Light
◡		882	945	Tawny

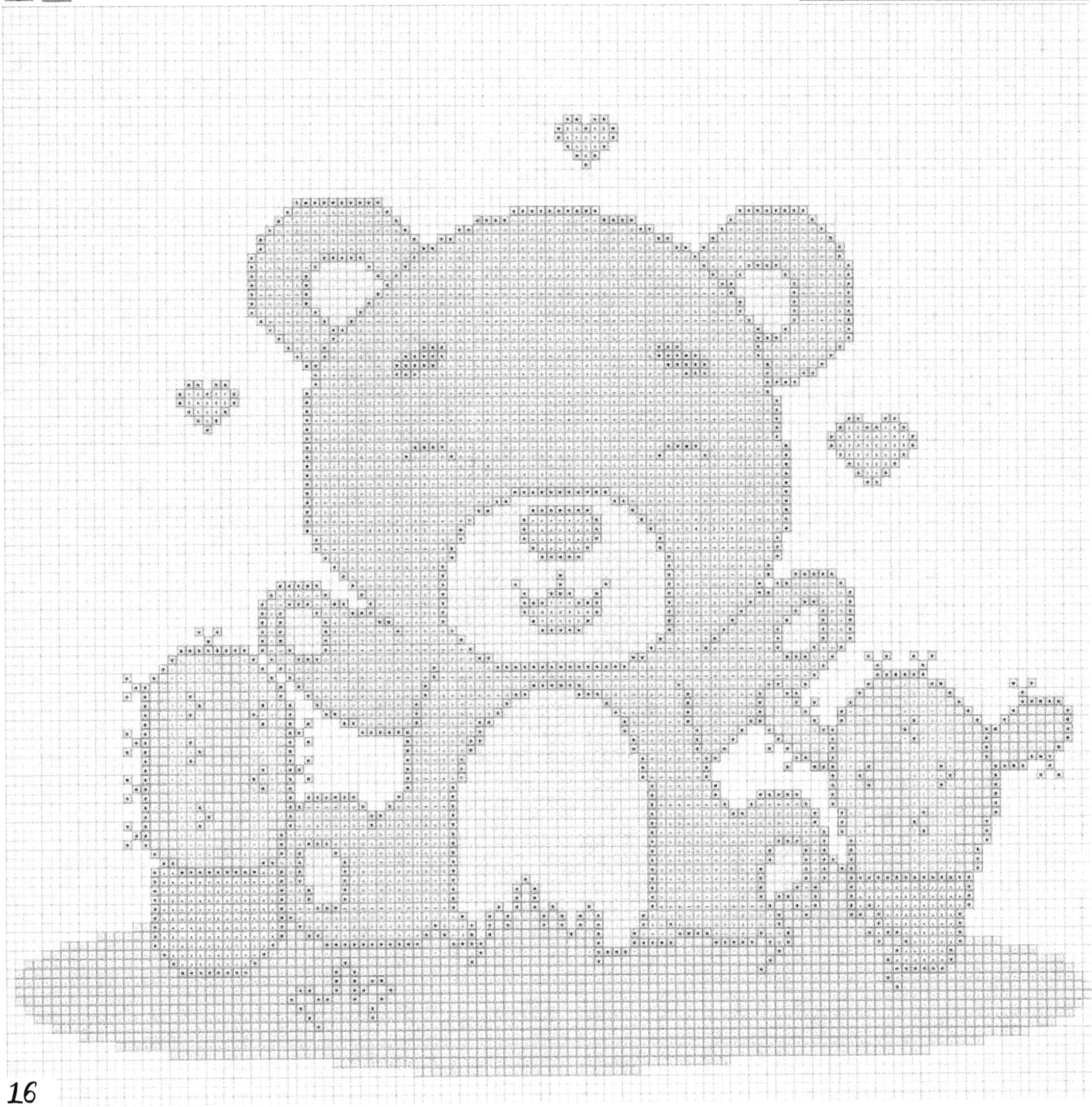

Lion

		Count	Code	Name
★		855	898	Coffee Brown Vy Dk
⊡		1670	3776	Mahogany Light
▲		3896	742	Tangerine Light
⊞		42	893	Carnation Light
⌘		76	3856	Mahogany Ult Vy Lt
∪		6	White	White

Unicorn on a pink flamingo

		Count	Code	Name
★		934	154	Grape Very Dark
▢		1855	603	Cranberry
▲		258	3609	Plum Ultra Light
✚		458	3708	Melon Light
☰		3212	727	Topaz Vy Lt
⊗		1053	162	Blue Ultra Very Light
◡		887	White	White

Fairy with a magic wand

		Count	Code	Name
★	■	720	310	Black
⊡	☐	112	307	Lemon
▲	☐	1296	3811	Turquoise Very Light
⊞	☐	340	827	Blue Very Light
◈	☐	1386	605	Cranberry Very Light
⌘	☐	174	211	Lavender Light
▤	☐	809	819	Baby Pink Light

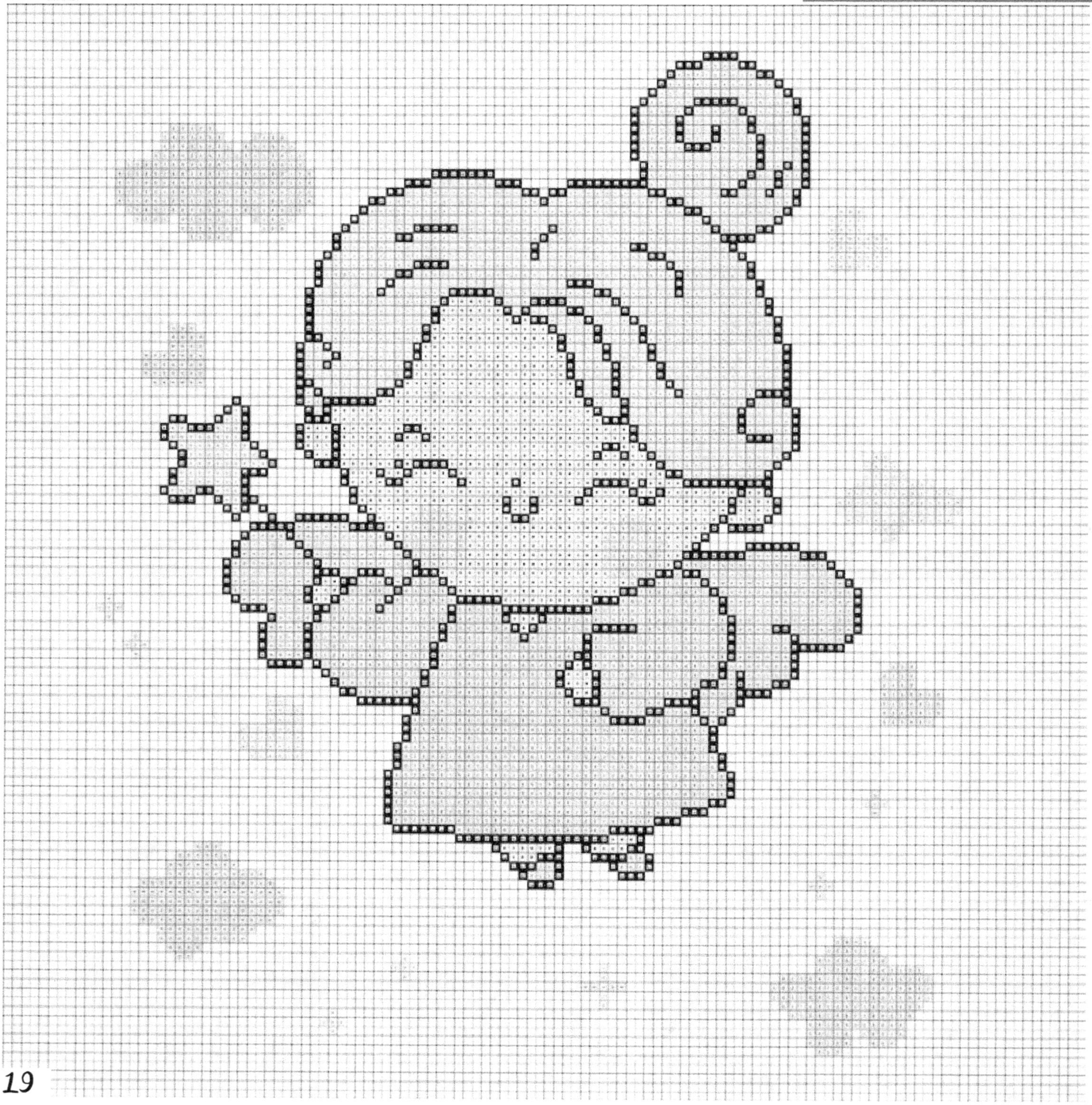

Unicorn holding a flower

		Count	Code	Name
★	■	838	310	Black
⊟		294	959	Sea Green Med
▲		2992	3609	Plum Ultra Light
＋		462	605	Cranberry Very Light
☰		1011	828	Sky Blue Vy Lt
⊠		474	727	Topaz Vy Lt
◖		6	3713	Salmon Very Light
∪		1658	White	White

Mermaid princess with a star

		Count	Code	Name
★	■	993	310	Black
⊡		2362	3772	Desert Sand Vy Dk
▲		214	3733	Dusty Rose
⊞		128	340	Blue Violet Medium
⌛		1062	445	Lemon Light
◆		213	605	Cranberry Very Light
☰		248	828	Sky Blue Vy Lt
◡		1039	819	Baby Pink Light

Tooth Fairy

		Count	Code	Name
★	■	775	310	Black
+		1356	3862	Mocha Beige Dark
▲		380	210	Lavender Medium
⊠		91	726	Topaz Light
≡		187	760	Salmon
⊃		423	828	Sky Blue Vy Lt
⌘		634	819	Baby Pink Light
⌣		1030	White	White

Mermaid with a heart

		Count	Code	Name
★	■	984	310	Black
□		1791	352	Coral Light
▲		383	3766	Peacock Blue Light
+		238	554	Violet Light
⊻		324	3689	Mauve Light
Σ		191	745	Yellow Pale Light
≡		96	162	Blue Ultra Very Light
⌣		1259	819	Baby Pink Light

Mermaid princess with a cup

		Count	Code	Name
★		704	550	Violet Very Dark
		1912	335	Rose
▲		375	597	Turquoise
		377	959	Sea Green Med
		92	210	Lavender Medium
		72	307	Lemon
		156	603	Cranberry
		103	964	Sea Green Light
		1134	3761	Sky Blue Light
		829	819	Baby Pink Light
		1182	White	White

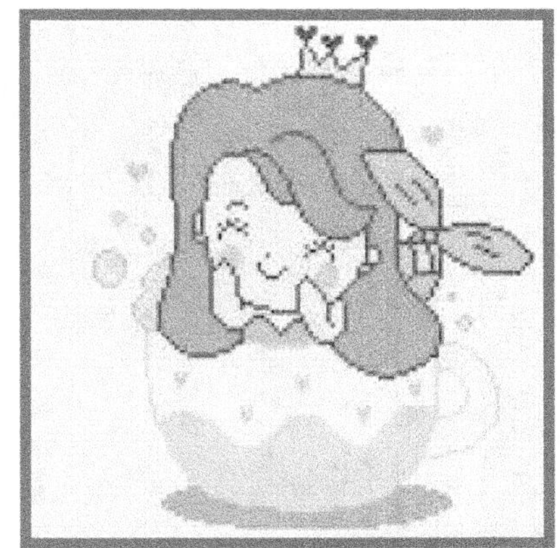

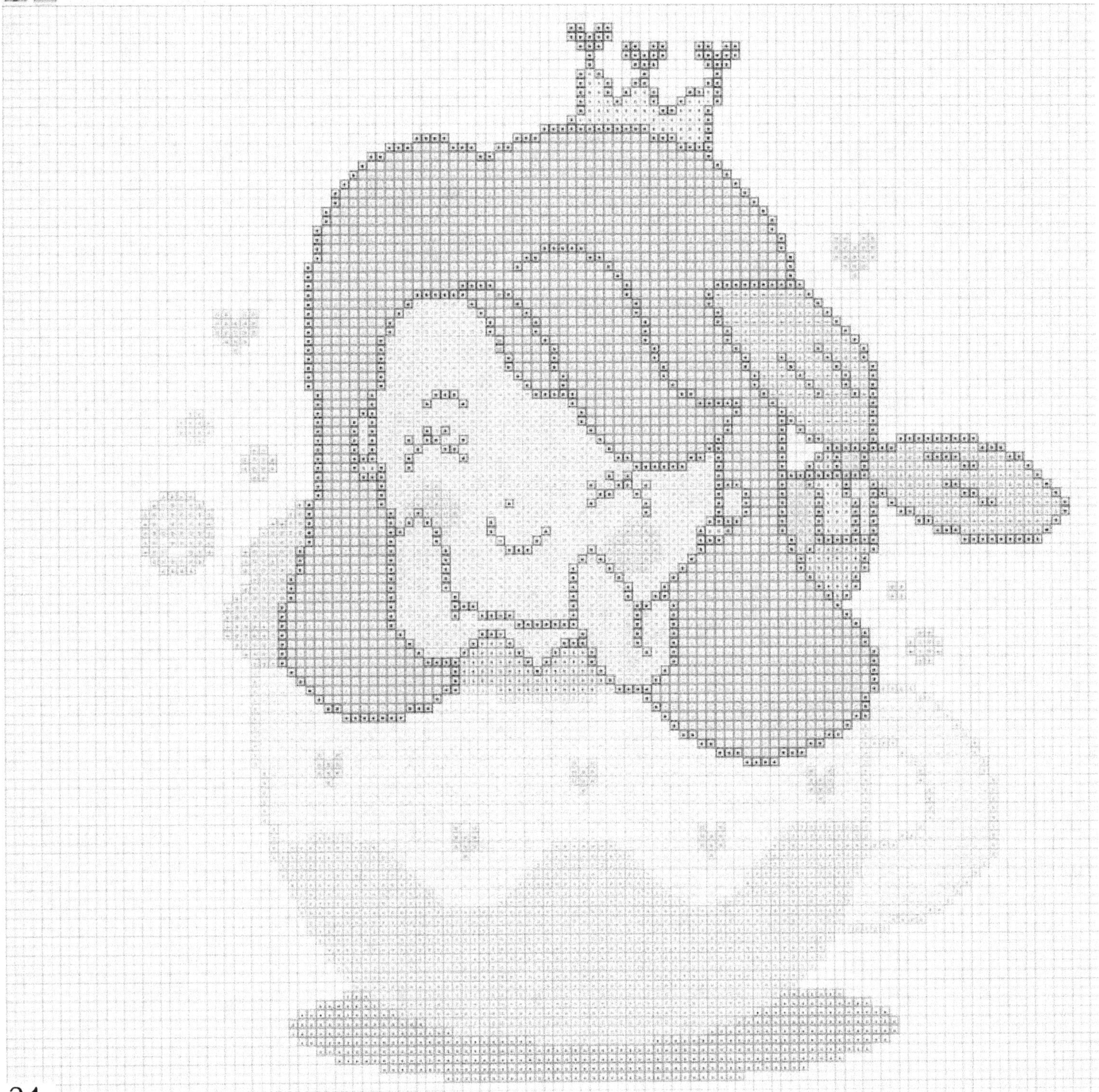

Little girl holding a baby unicorn

		Count	Code	Name
★		813	3777	Terra Cotta Vy Dk
▢		46	3341	Apricot
▲		152	3608	Plum Very Light
⊞		67	3822	Straw Light
⌘		356	504	Blue Green Vy Lt
▤		174	453	Shell Gray Light
◆		1725	3708	Melon Light
⌣		982	712	Cream

Pilot unicorn fly on an airplane

	Count	Code	Name
★	732	535	Ash Gray Vy Lt
⊡	962	519	Sky Blue
▲	302	893	Carnation Light
⊗	113	554	Violet Light
⊠	168	504	Blue Green Vy Lt
≡	1400	445	Lemon Light
✖	500	605	Cranberry Very Light
⊞	46	762	Pearl Gray Vy Lt
⌣	1128	White	White

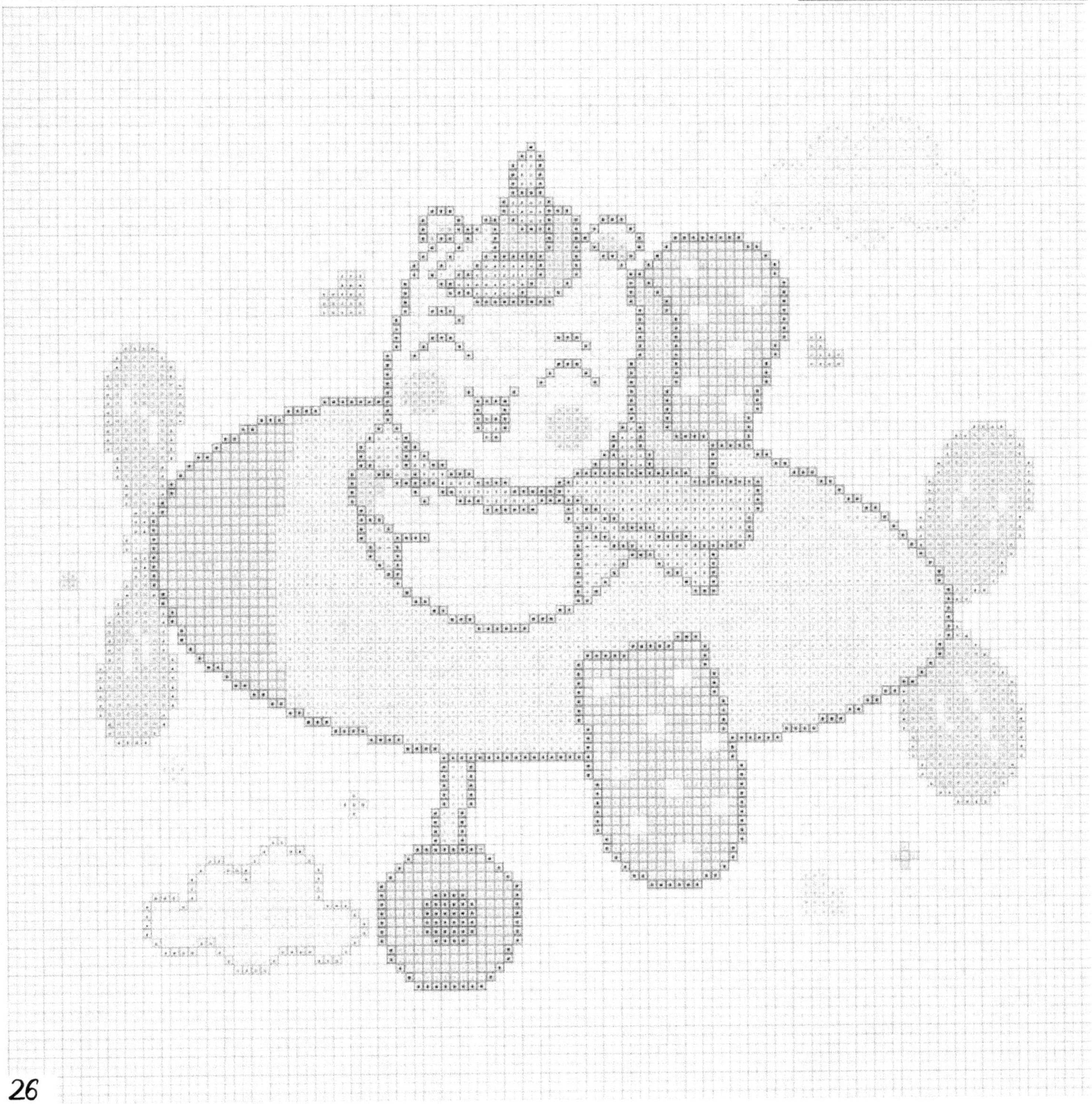

Unicorn sleeping on a cloud

		Count	Code	Name
★		1371	718	Plum
▫		276	598	Turquoise Light
▲		231	210	Lavender Medium
◆		58	341	Blue Violet Light
┼		446	3609	Plum Ultra Light
⌘		296	445	Lemon Light
⌶		286	827	Blue Very Light
▤		299	963	Dusty Rose Ult Vy Lt
⌣		3491	White	White

Princess with a unicorn whale

		Count	Code	Name
★		772	898	Coffee Brown Vy Dk
⊞		639	632	Desert Sand Ult Vy Dk
▲		183	322	Baby Blue Dark
▤		515	3716	Dusty Rose Med Vy Lt
⌘		175	744	Yellow Pale
⚡		2950	827	Blue Very Light
⊗		376	819	Baby Pink Light
◡		288	White	White

Caticorn on a cloud

Count	Code	Name
817	550	Violet Very Dark
74	893	Carnation Light
196	743	Yellow Med
271	554	Violet Light
2068	828	Sky Blue Vy Lt
130	3708	Melon Light
61	727	Topaz Vy Lt
1169	White	White

Unicorn girl holding a strawberry cupcake

		Count	Code	Name
★		965	550	Violet Very Dark
⊡		66	892	Carnation Medium
▲		132	743	Yellow Med
⊞		550	603	Cranberry
⊓		168	964	Sea Green Light
⊠		177	445	Lemon Light
◆		640	211	Lavender Light
☰		267	3841	Baby Blue Pale
⌘		467	963	Dusty Rose Ult Vy Lt
⌣		754	3866	Mocha Brn Ult Vy Lt

Pegasus flying on pastel sky

		Count	Code	Name
★	■	757	814	Garnet Dark
▫		947	3609	Plum Ultra Light
▲		637	211	Lavender Light
+		1348	828	Sky Blue Vy Lt
☰		873	727	Topaz Vy Lt
✕		143	963	Dusty Rose Ult Vy Lt
⊗		2338	747	Peacock Blue Vy Lt
⌣		1947	White	White

Princess with a pony

		Count	Code	Name
★		912	814	Garnet Dark
⊡		866	167	Yellow Beige V Dk
▲		174	307	Lemon
△		111	341	Blue Violet Light
⊞		627	603	Cranberry
◈		294	453	Shell Gray Light
⊘		130	3609	Plum Ultra Light
☰		431	605	Cranberry Very Light
⌘		376	819	Baby Pink Light
⌣		542	White	White

Unicorn with donuts

		Count	Code	Name
★		809	814	Garnet Dark
⊞		778	304	Red Medium
▲		100	307	Lemon
⋈		202	3608	Plum Very Light
⌘		630	3825	Pumpkin Pale
≣		48	472	Avocado Grn U Lt
◆		815	604	Cranberry Light
⊗		418	963	Dusty Rose Ult Vy Lt
⌣		1406	White	White

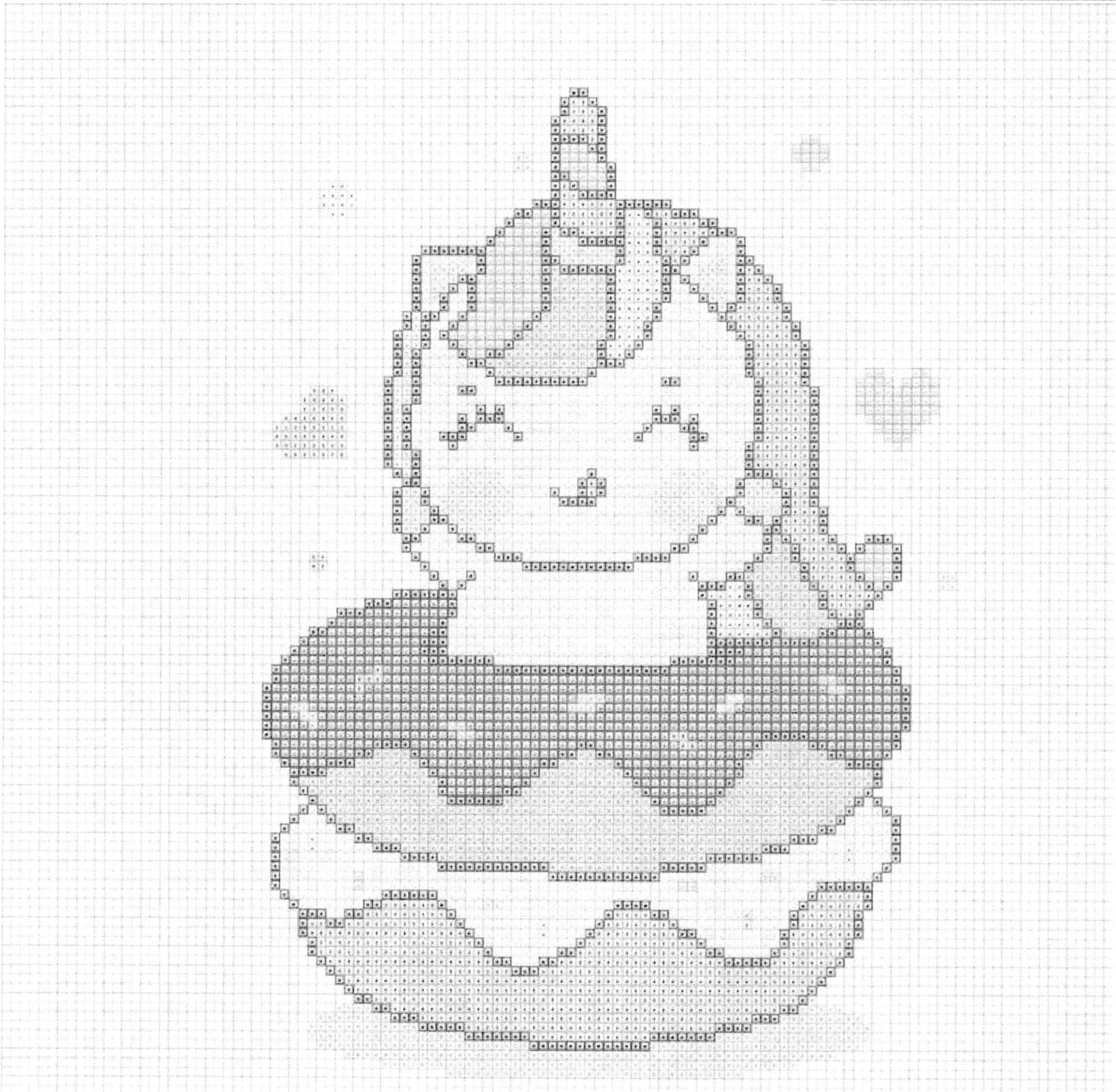

Unicorn eating a strawberry ice cream

		Count	Code	Name
★		858	3371	Black Brown
▫		139	891	Carnation Dark
▲		85	210	Lavender Medium
┼		1012	3806	Cyclamen Pink Light
≣		889	3822	Straw Light
⌘		91	445	Lemon Light
◆		245	605	Cranberry Very Light
⌣		1239	White	White

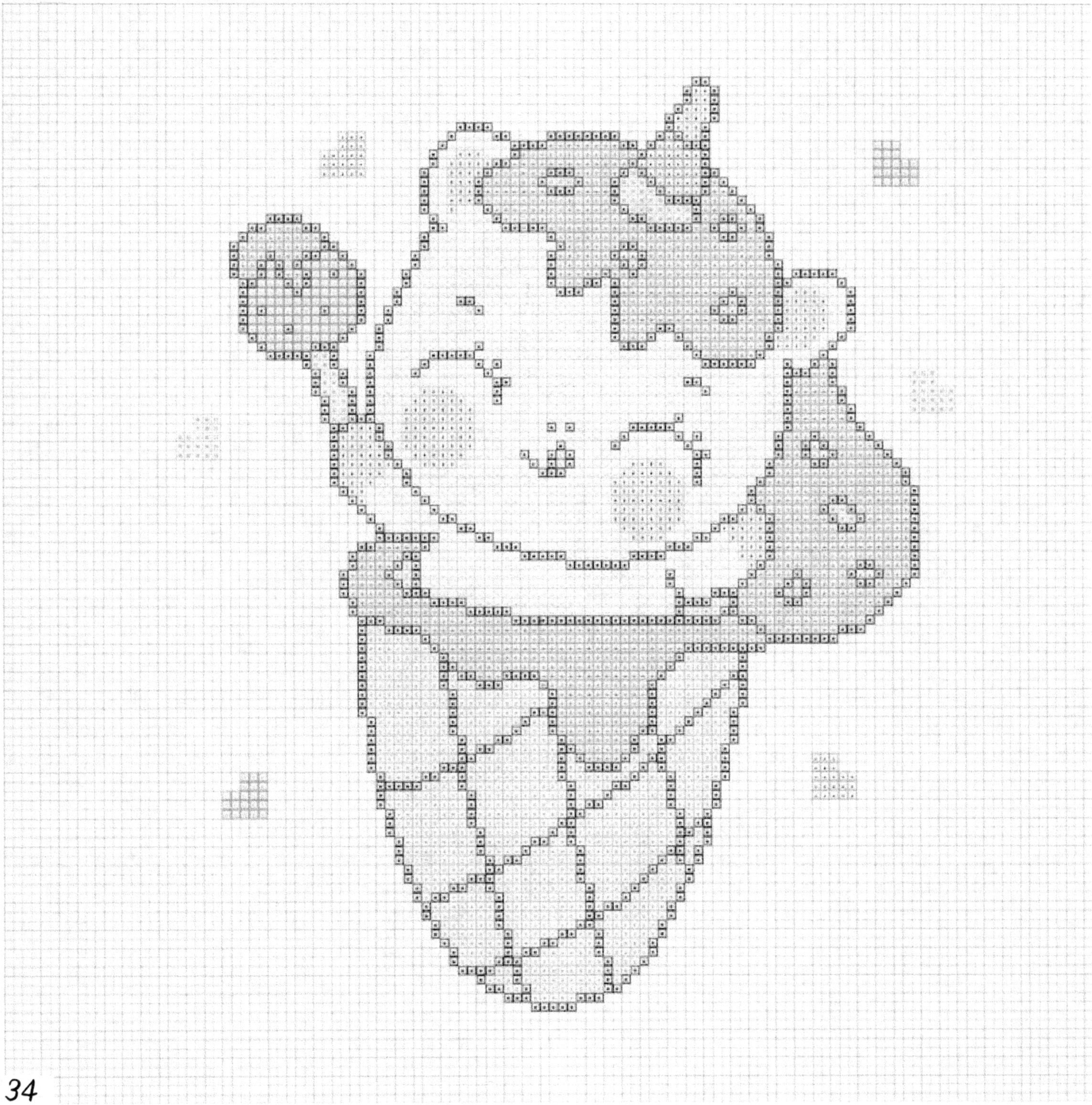

Unicorn on sweet cherry and strawberry cake

	Count	Code	Name
★	700	550	Violet Very Dark
□	634	3801	Melon Very Dark
▲	32	704	Chartreuse Bright
⊞	98	972	Canary Deep
⌘	547	210	Lavender Medium
≣	466	760	Salmon
◆	1171	554	Violet Light
⊗	794	445	Lemon Light
⌣	910	White	White

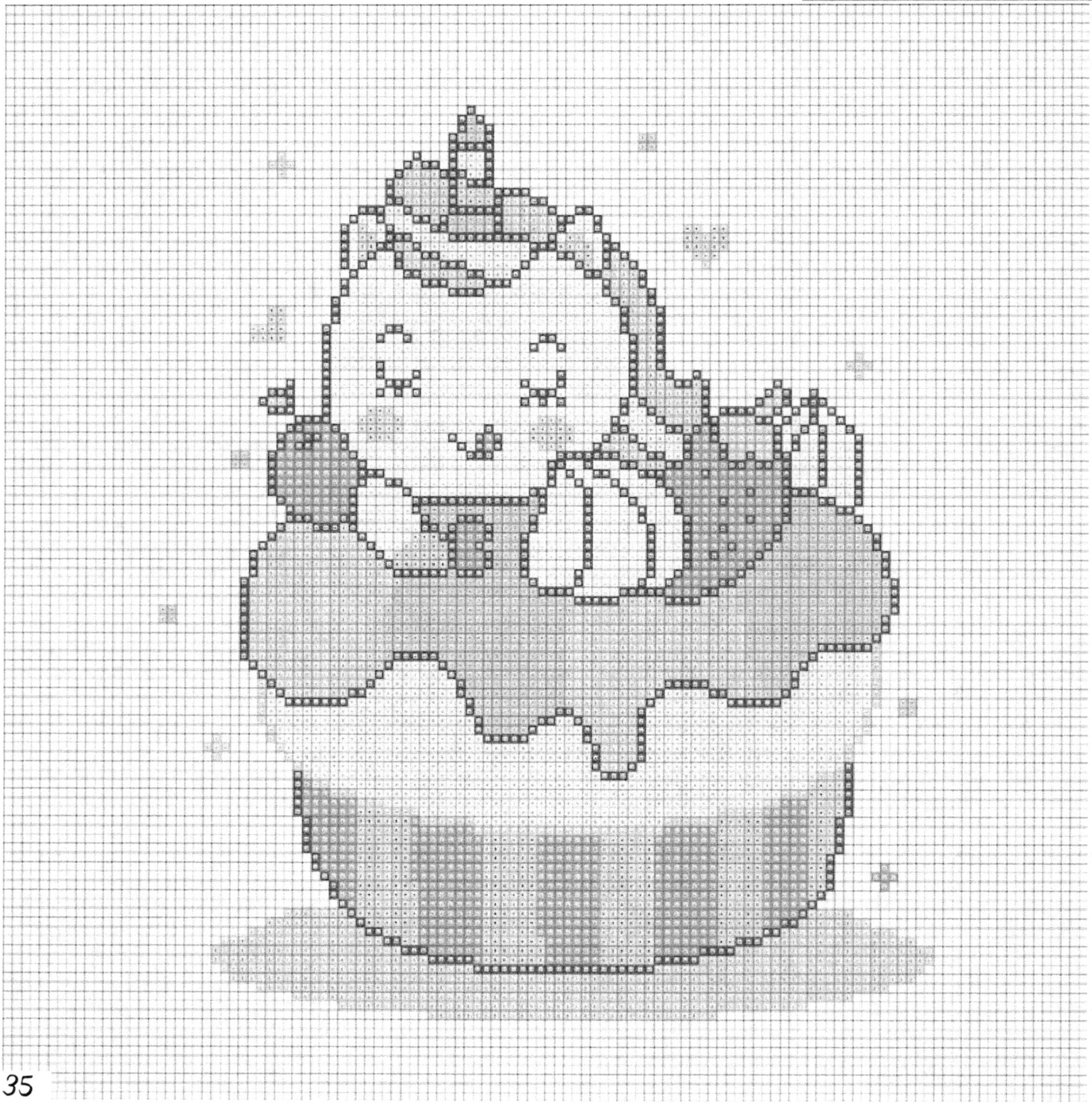

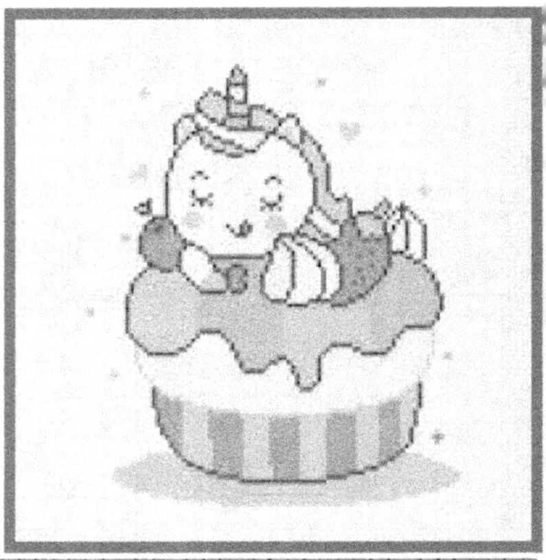

Pony wearing Santa hat

		Count	Code	Name
★		928	898	Coffee Brown Vy Dk
▫		58	959	Sea Green Med
▲		138	210	Lavender Medium
☰		997	603	Cranberry
⊞		536	964	Sea Green Light
ⓧ		294	445	Lemon Light
⌘		1156	818	Baby Pink
⌣		1570	White	White

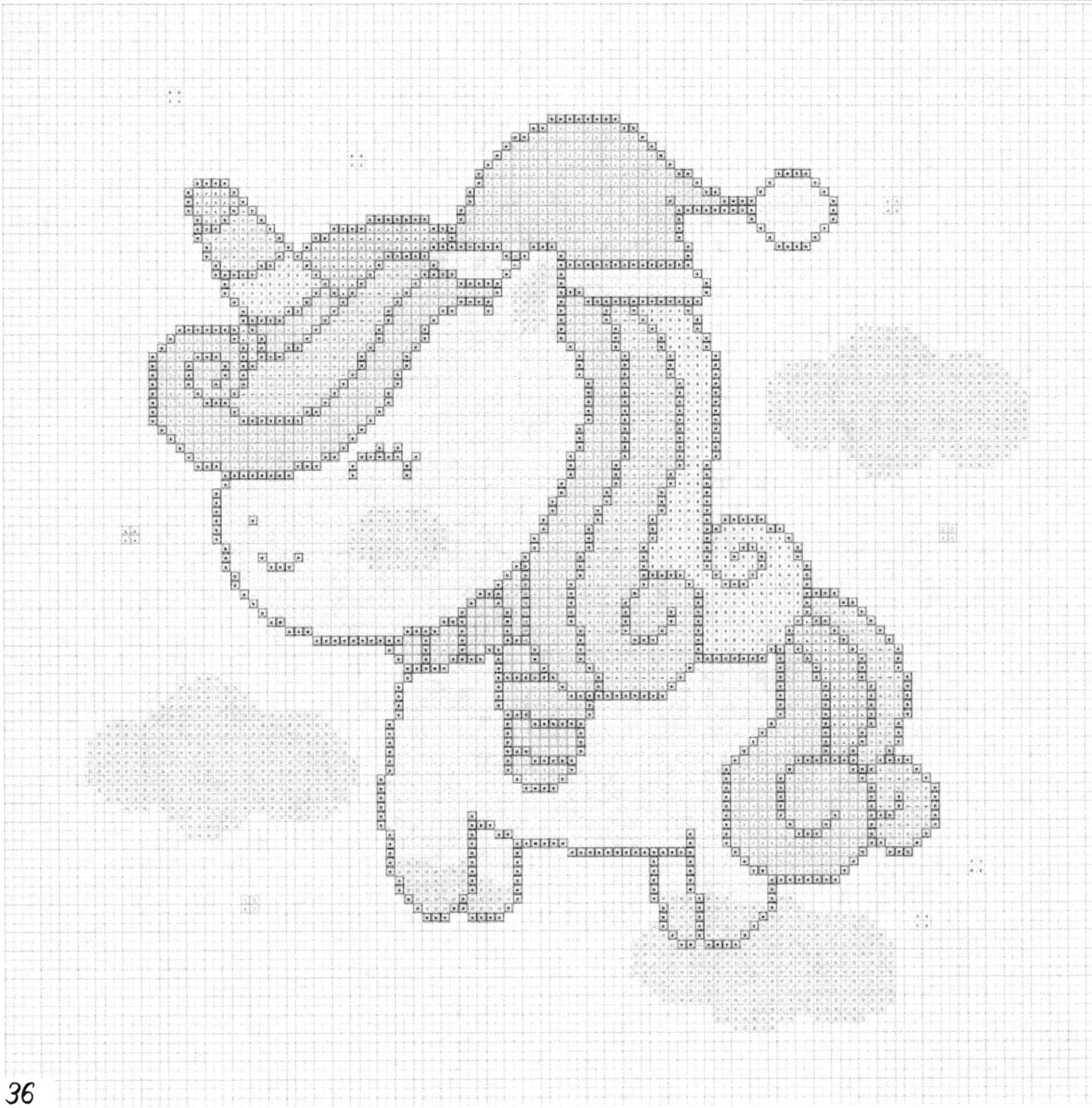

Unicorn eating a yummy donut

		Count	Code	Name
★		995	898	Coffee Brown Vy Dk
⊡		679	372	Mustard Lt
▲		726	3608	Plum Very Light
⌘		770	3326	Rose Light
►		99	504	Blue Green Vy Lt
+		599	744	Yellow Pale
⊠		360	211	Lavender Light
▤		206	3708	Melon Light
⊗		444	928	Gray Green Vy Lt
◡		2221	White	White

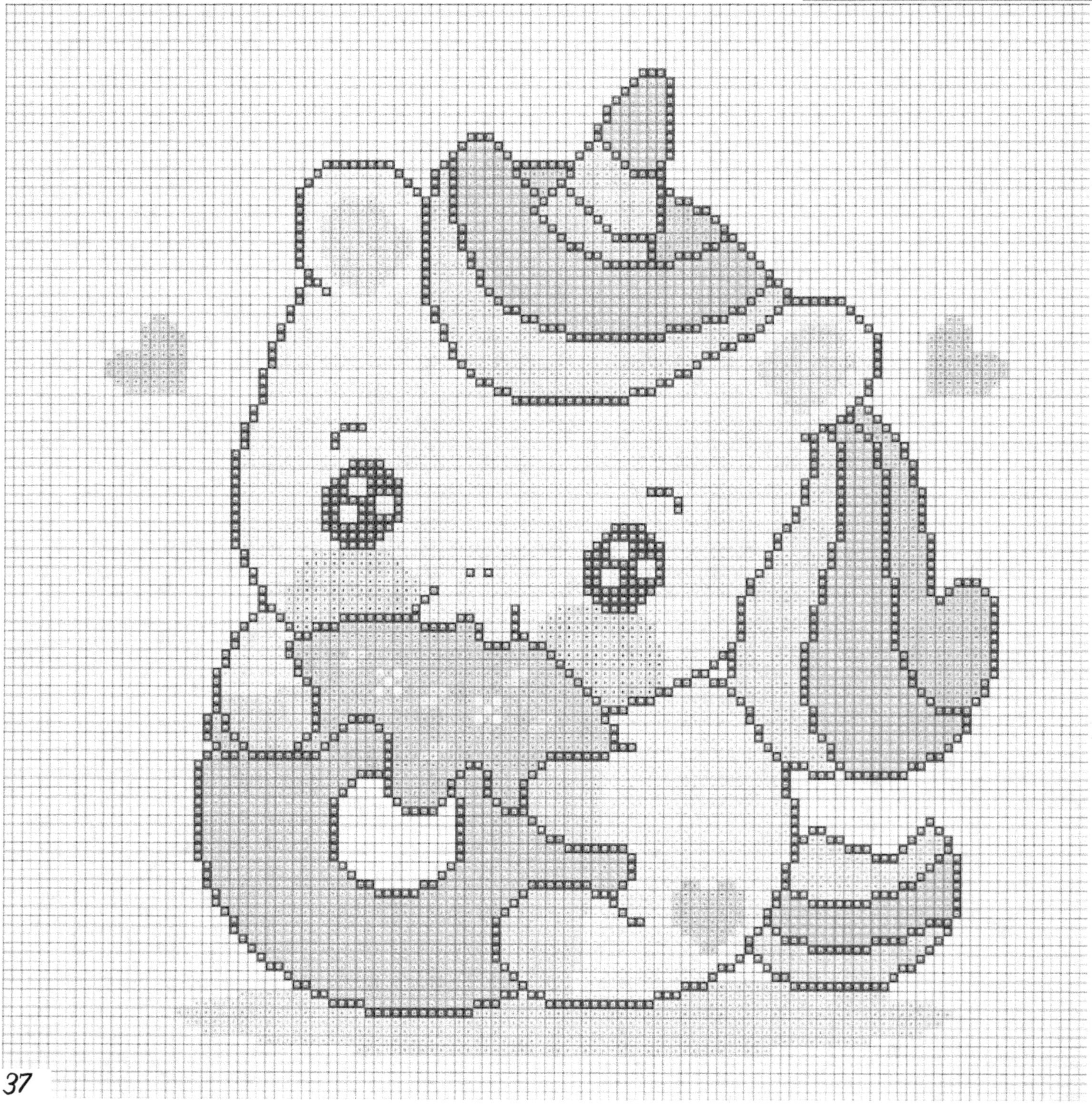

Unicorn on a cotton candy

		Count	Code	Name
★		826	814	Garnet Dark
▫		524	3608	Plum Very Light
▲		139	504	Blue Green Vy Lt
+		217	744	Yellow Pale
≡		1941	605	Cranberry Very Light
⊼		215	928	Gray Green Vy Lt
∪		1274	White	White

Caticorn fish holding a star

		Count	Code	Name
★		663	791	Cornflower Blue V D
□		182	341	Blue Violet Light
▲		83	472	Avocado Grn U Lt
＋		230	964	Sea Green Light
⌘		196	3609	Plum Ultra Light
☰		261	744	Yellow Pale
⊗		80	3708	Melon Light
⌣		1554	White	White

Caticorn fish holding a balloon

		Count	Code	Name
★		653	791	Cornflower Blue V D
▣		412	341	Blue Violet Light
▲		124	472	Avocado Grn U Lt
⊞		216	964	Sea Green Light
⊠		311	3609	Plum Ultra Light
☰		194	744	Yellow Pale
⌘		58	3708	Melon Light
⌣		1161	White	White

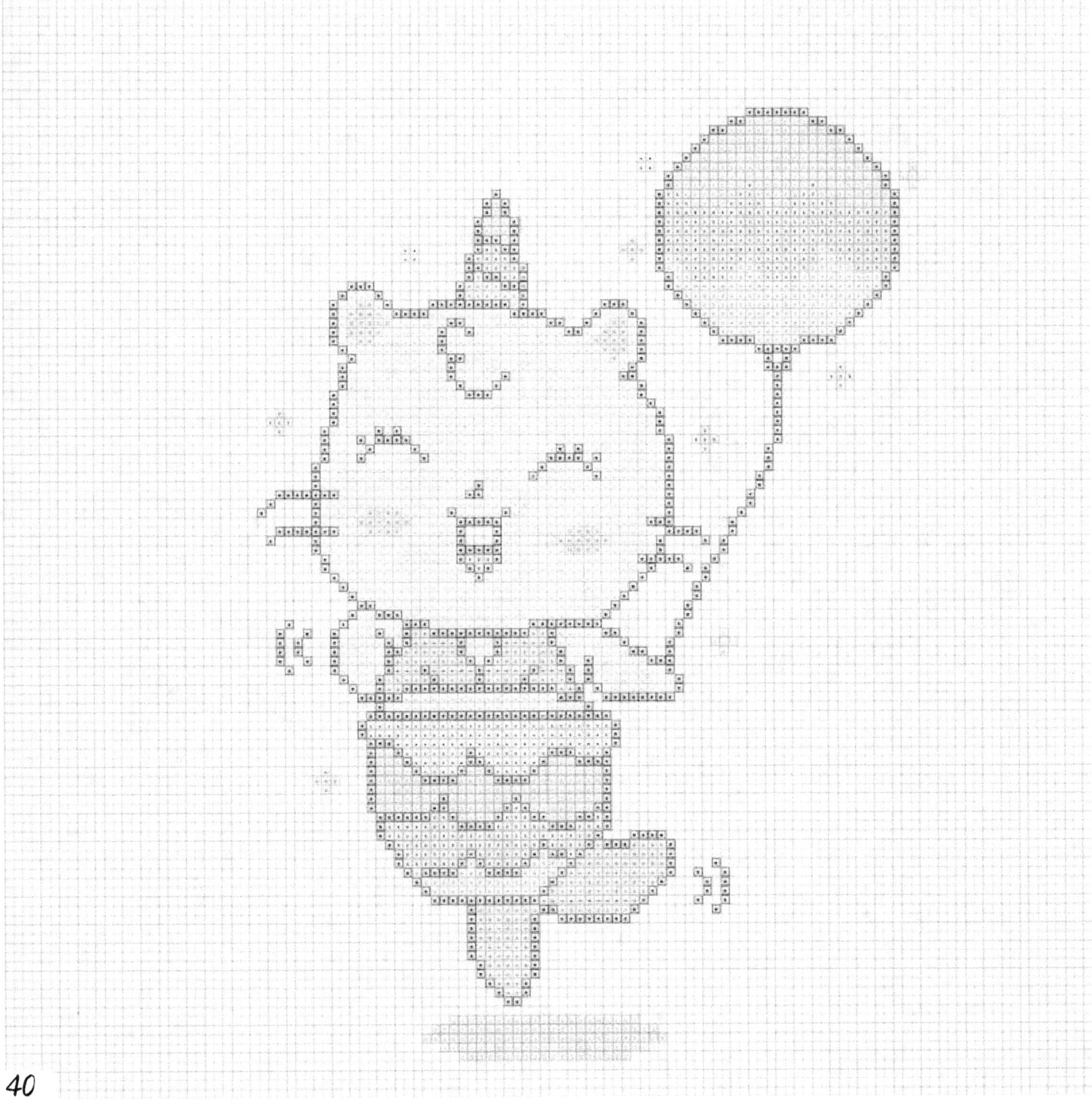

Unicorn on the moon

		Count	Code	Name
★		718	792	Cornflower Blue Dark
⊡		83	472	Avocado Grn U Lt
▲		1087	744	Yellow Pale
⊞		118	211	Lavender Light
☰		187	3841	Baby Blue Pale
⊠		1173	828	Sky Blue Vy Lt
⌘		209	3708	Melon Light
⌣		760	White	White

Unicorn dreaming on an ice cream

	Count	Code	Name
★	851	838	Beige Brown Vy Dk
⊡	240	210	Lavender Medium
▲	900	676	Old Gold Lt
⊞	641	604	Cranberry Light
⌘	64	504	Blue Green Vy Lt
⌶	92	3609	Plum Ultra Light
▤	153	761	Salmon Light
◈	201	727	Topaz Vy Lt
⌣	1007	White	White

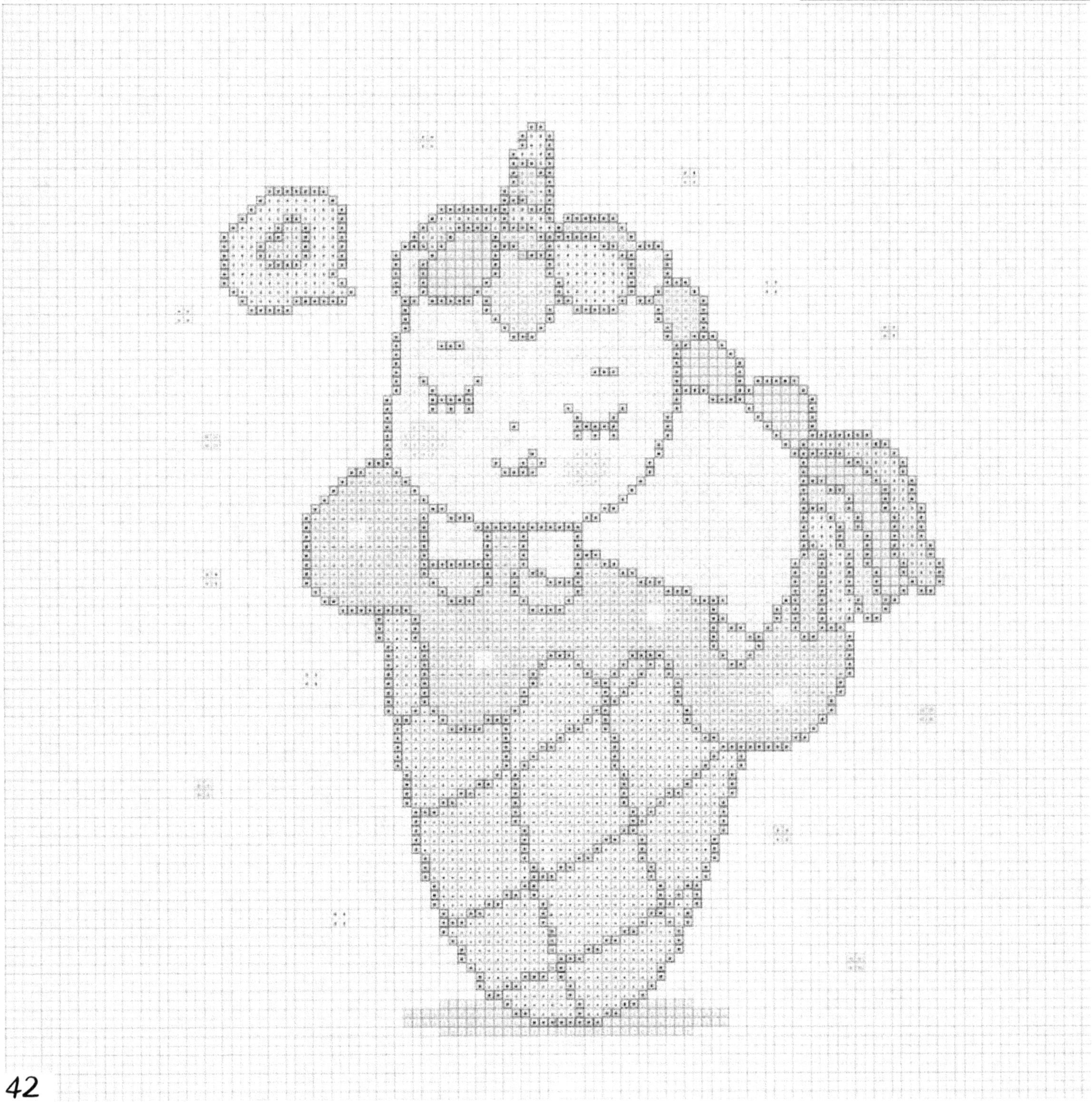

Unicorn's birthday cake

		Count	Code	Name
★		797	550	Violet Very Dark
⊡		103	368	Pistachio Green Lt
▲		287	210	Lavender Medium
⊞		248	893	Carnation Light
⌘		116	743	Yellow Med
⊠		343	964	Sea Green Light
▤		127	445	Lemon Light
◈		652	605	Cranberry Very Light
⌐		365	211	Lavender Light
◡		1305	White	White

Sleepy unicorn

		Count	Code	Name
★		726	158	Cornflower Blu M V D
⊡		1151	156	Blue Violet Med Lt
▲		190	605	Cranberry Very Light
⊞		211	211	Lavender Light
≡		468	745	Yellow Pale Light
⊠		130	3747	Blue Violet Vy Lt
⌘		673	828	Sky Blue Vy Lt
⌣		1253	White	White

Kids

		Count	Code	Name
★		1340	939	Navy Blue Very Dark
⊟		455	680	Old Gold Dark
▲		243	825	Blue Dark
＋		255	3851	Green Bright Lt
⌘		140	3805	Cyclamen Pink
◆		221	444	Lemon Dark
▼		686	3340	Apricot Med
⊑		287	603	Cranberry
⊡		523	928	Gray Green Vy Lt
☰		1187	3713	Salmon Very Light
⌣		56	White	White

Baby with a yellow duck

		Count	Code	Name
★		91	3371	Black Brown
⊡		46	922	Copper Light
▲		349	972	Canary Deep
⊼		914	444	Lemon Dark
⊞		324	758	Terra Cotta Vy Lt
⊕		72	3706	Melon Medium
⌘		3151	353	Peach
▤		79	762	Pearl Gray Vy Lt
⌣		196	White	White

Baby girl

		Count	Code	Name
★		68	3371	Black Brown
▫		274	3778	Terra Cotta Light
▲		336	3705	Melon Dark
┼		210	307	Lemon
✗		564	3608	Plum Very Light
▤		3085	3825	Pumpkin Pale
⌘		640	3708	Melon Light
‿		54	White	White

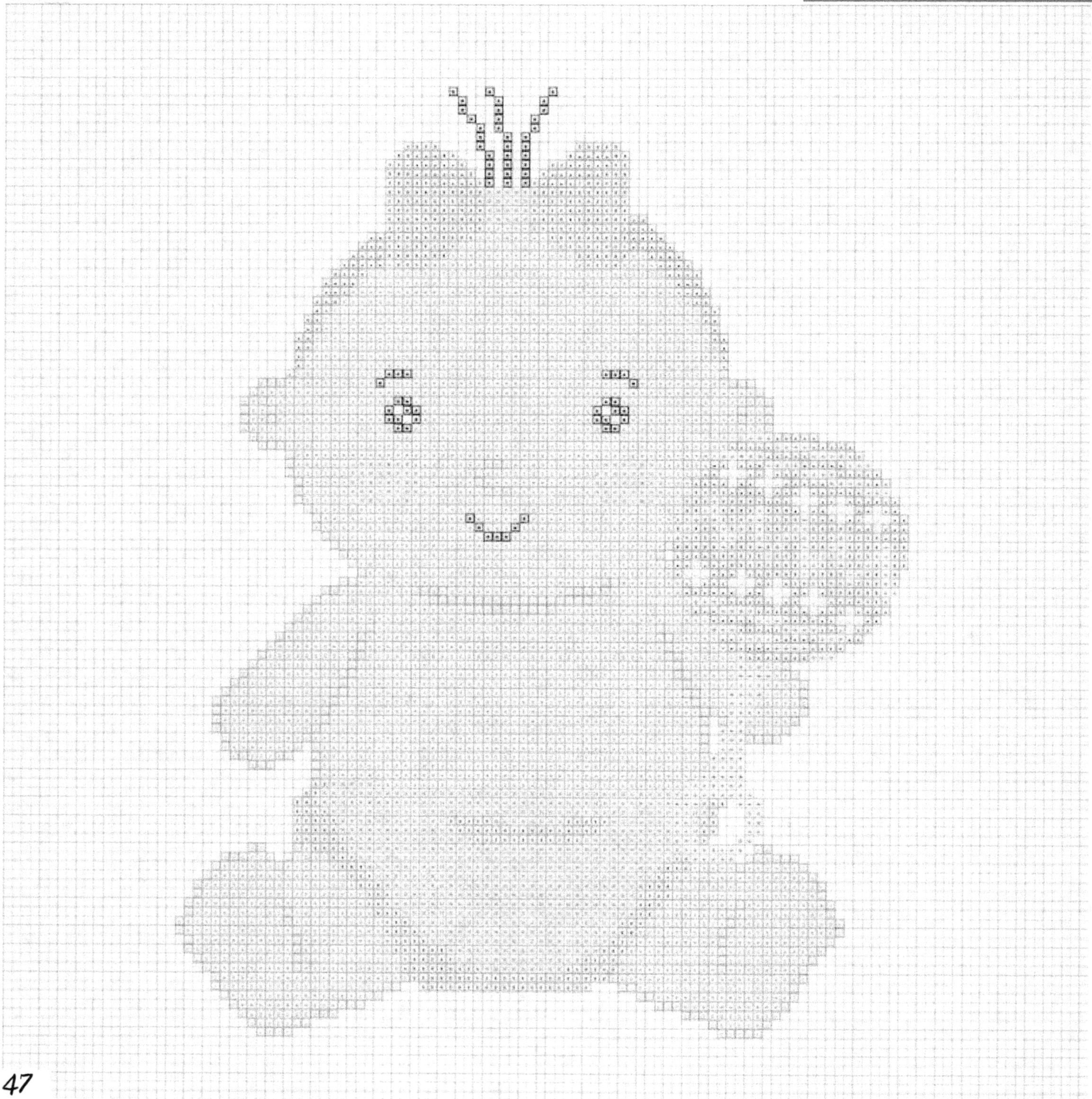

Baby boy

		Count	Code	Name
★		139	3371	Black Brown
⊡		814	939	Navy Blue Very Dark
▲		606	3843	Electric Blue
⊞		39	3801	Melon Very Dark
≡		303	3778	Terra Cotta Light
⌶		595	3766	Peacock Blue Light
⌘		2516	3825	Pumpkin Pale
⌣		15	White	White

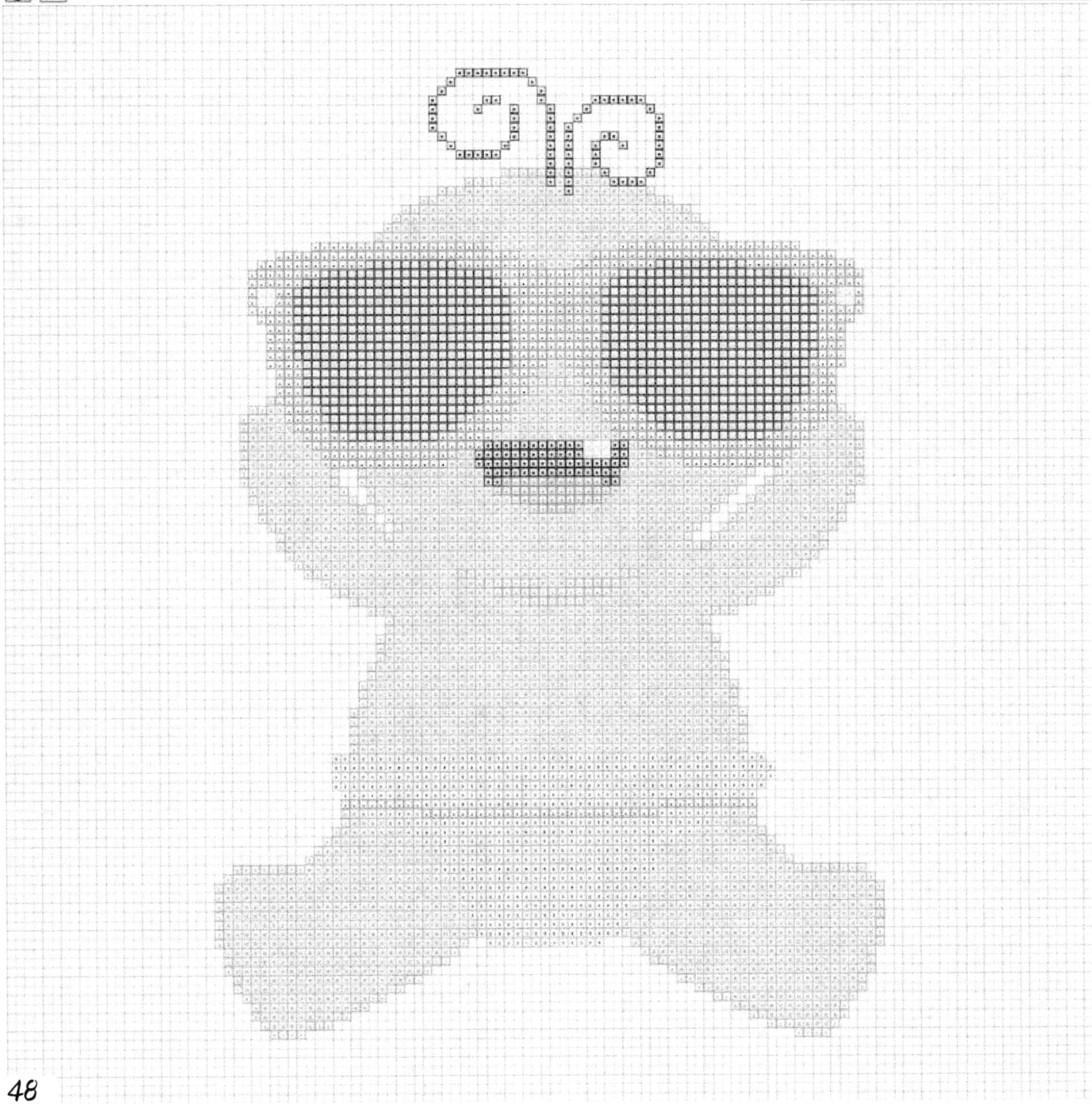

	Count	Code	Name
★	726	938	Coffee Brown Ult Dk
□	239	905	Parrot Green Dk
▲	288	347	Salmon Very Dark
☰	1919	704	Chartreuse Bright
⊼	280	436	Tan
+	53	415	Pearl Gray
∪	86	White	White

Gasteria succulent plant

		Count	Code	Name
★		806	934	Avocado Grn Black
▢		1035	501	Blue Green Dark
▲		1547	562	Jade Medium
⊞		14	335	Rose
▤		615	977	Golden Brown Light
⌘		1492	3827	Golden Brown Pale
⌧		34	761	Salmon Light
⌣		201	White	White

Mom and baby cactus

		Count	Code	Name
★		795	934	Avocado Grn Black
⊡		2164	562	Jade Medium
▲		21	335	Rose
⊞		74	3733	Dusty Rose
⊔		234	402	Mahogany Vy Lt
⊠		197	955	Nile Green Light
◈		2360	3766	Peacock Blue Light
☰		235	3326	Rose Light
⌣		32	White	White

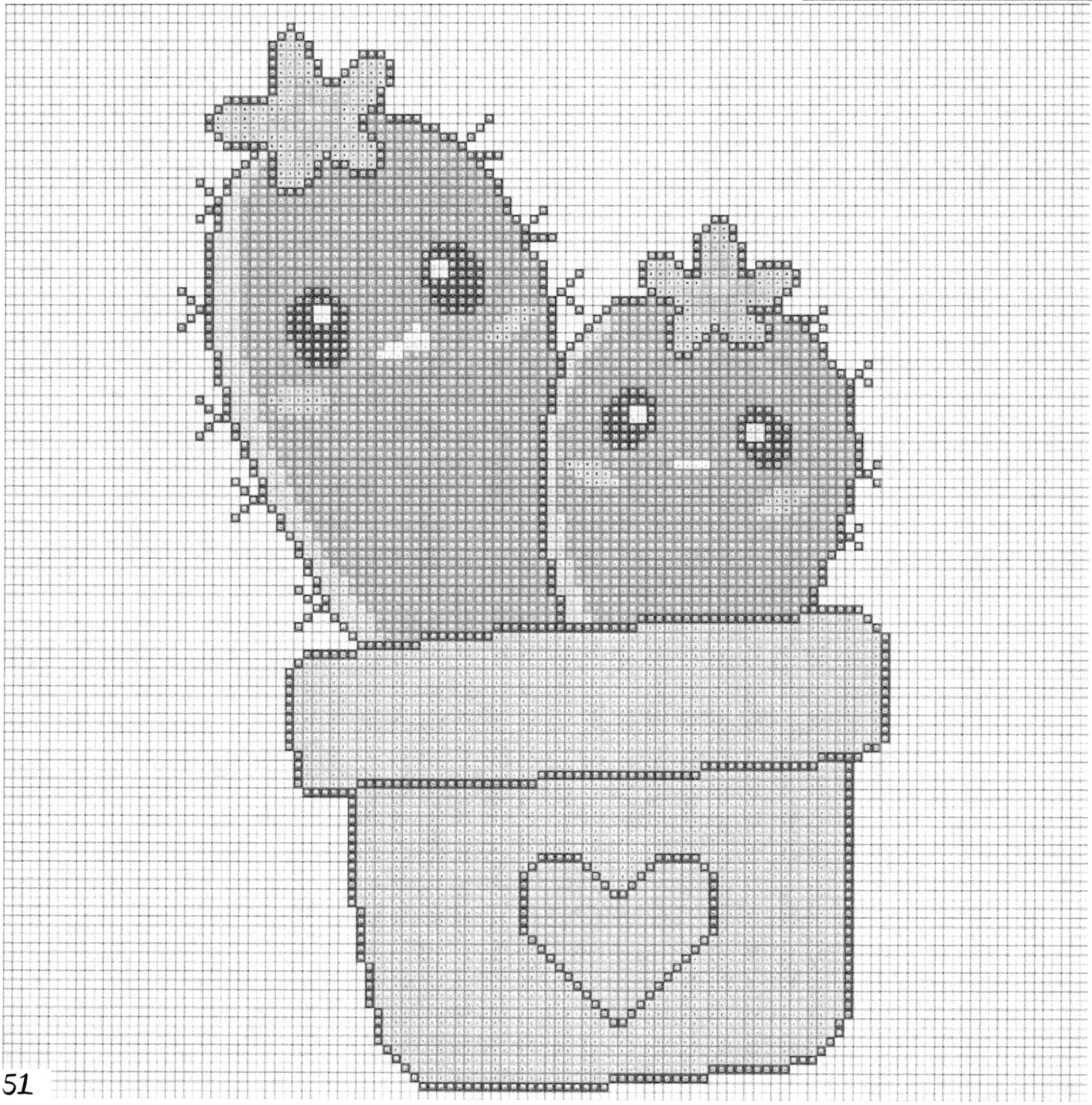

Rainbow and clouds

		Count	Code	Name
★		57	154	Grape Very Dark
▫		349	3844	Turquoise Bright Dark
▲		616	3801	Melon Very Dark
⊞		260	161	Blue Gray
⌘		58	3731	Dusty Rose Very Dark
∃		576	3853	Autumn Gold Dk
☆		383	471	Avocado Grn V Lt
◆		489	725	Topaz Med Lt
⊗		599	950	Desert Sand Light
⌒		1521	White	White

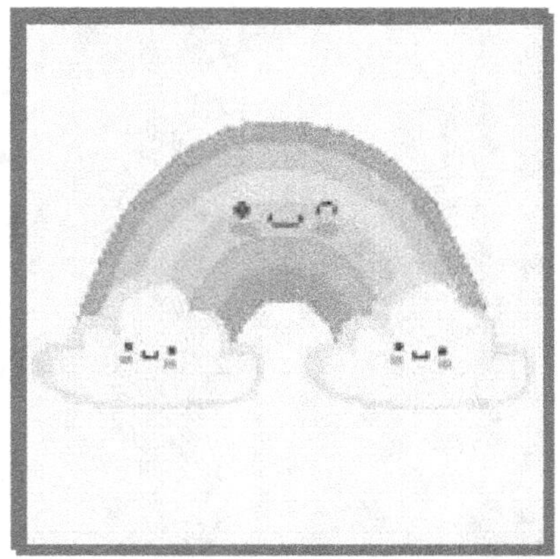

Flying rainbow cloud

		Count	Code	Name
★		42	796	Royal Blue Dark
⊞		541	666	Bright Red
▲		345	3807	Cornflower Blue
✕		281	995	Electric Blue Dark
◆		306	704	Chartreuse Bright
Ǝ		389	721	Orange Spice Med
⋈		425	725	Topaz Med Lt
▯		20	3733	Dusty Rose
≡		1873	3761	Sky Blue Light

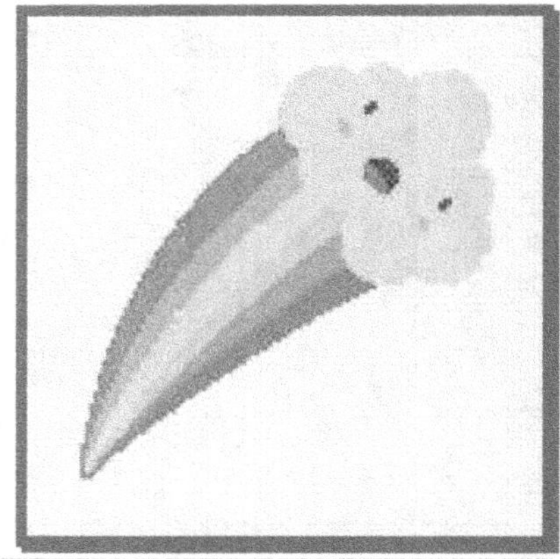

Rainbow love heart

		Count	Code	Name
★		22	796	Royal Blue Dark
☐		66	3837	Lavender Ultra Dark
▲		900	702	Kelly Green
⌘		438	312	Baby Blue Very Dark
◆		286	666	Bright Red
▤		986	922	Copper Light
⊕		996	444	Lemon Dark
✗		22	3733	Dusty Rose
⊞		1511	3761	Sky Blue Light

Mother earth

		Count	Code	Name
★		921	898	Coffee Brown Vy Dk
⊡		195	905	Parrot Green Dk
▲		440	702	Kelly Green
⊞		609	906	Parrot Green Md
✵		465	995	Electric Blue Dark
⊠		185	704	Chartreuse Bright
☰		1362	959	Sea Green Med
⊗		92	760	Salmon
◆		644	3761	Sky Blue Light
⌣		600	White	White

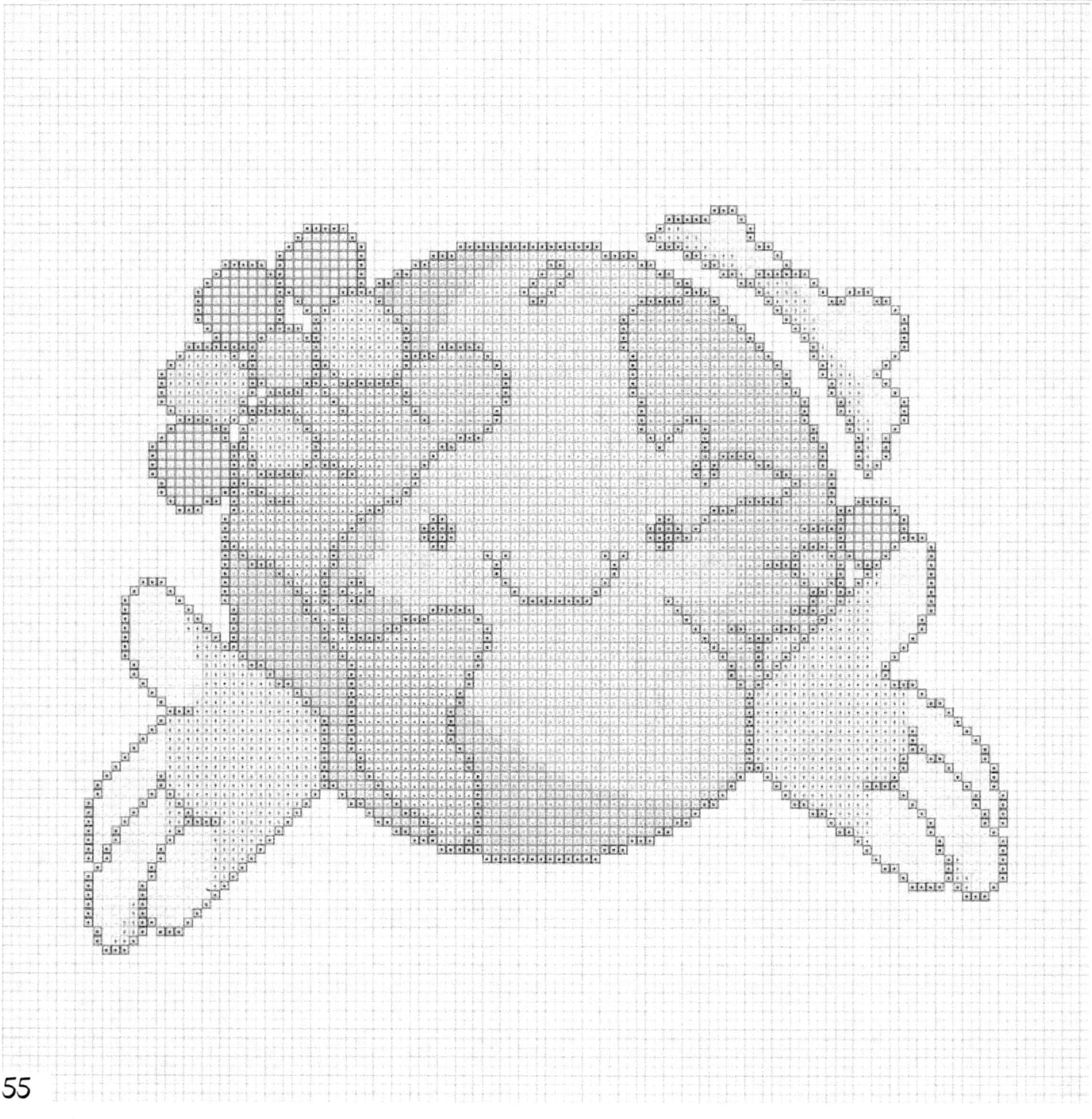

Smiley flower

		Count	Code	Name
★	■	735	310	Black
▫		91	702	Kelly Green
▲		237	3805	Cyclamen Pink
✕		514	996	Electric Blue Medium
+		707	973	Canary Bright
≡		820	3806	Cyclamen Pink Light
◡		14	White	White

Unicorn climbing the Christmas tree

	Count	Code	Name
★	795	898	Coffee Brown Vy Dk
	559	912	Emerald Green Lt
▲	186	350	Coral Medium
⊞	846	703	Chartreuse
	141	422	Hazelnut Brown Lt
◆	101	973	Canary Bright
	202	341	Blue Violet Light
	185	828	Sky Blue Vy Lt
	326	3708	Melon Light
	98	727	Topaz Vy Lt
	929	White	White

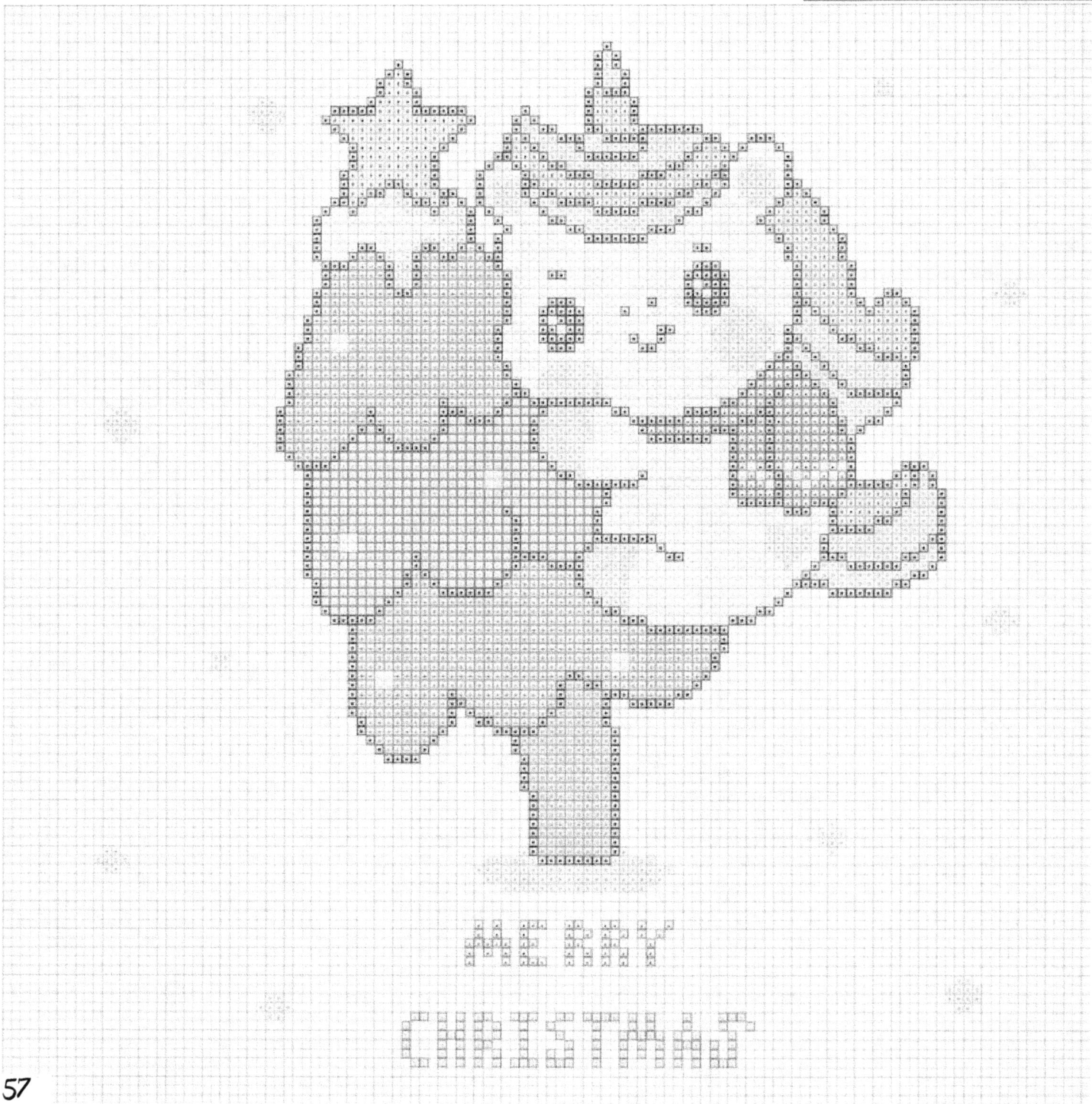

Girl and unicorn in a Christmas stocking

		Count	Code	Name
★		1015	898	Coffee Brown Vy Dk
⬚		1833	666	Bright Red
▲		277	3828	Hazelnut Brown
✕		246	959	Sea Green Med
▤		228	3819	Moss Green Lt
┼		510	3806	Cyclamen Pink Light
⊘		125	605	Cranberry Very Light
◆		183	819	Baby Pink Light
⌣		786	White	White

Reindeer sitting on a Christmas gift

		Count	Code	Name
★		973	938	Coffee Brown Ult Dk
⊡		118	433	Brown Med
▲		1469	666	Bright Red
⊞		263	420	Hazelnut Brown Dk
⊗		837	703	Chartreuse
⌘		823	436	Tan
◈		96	973	Canary Bright
▤		418	603	Cranberry
⌣		512	White	White

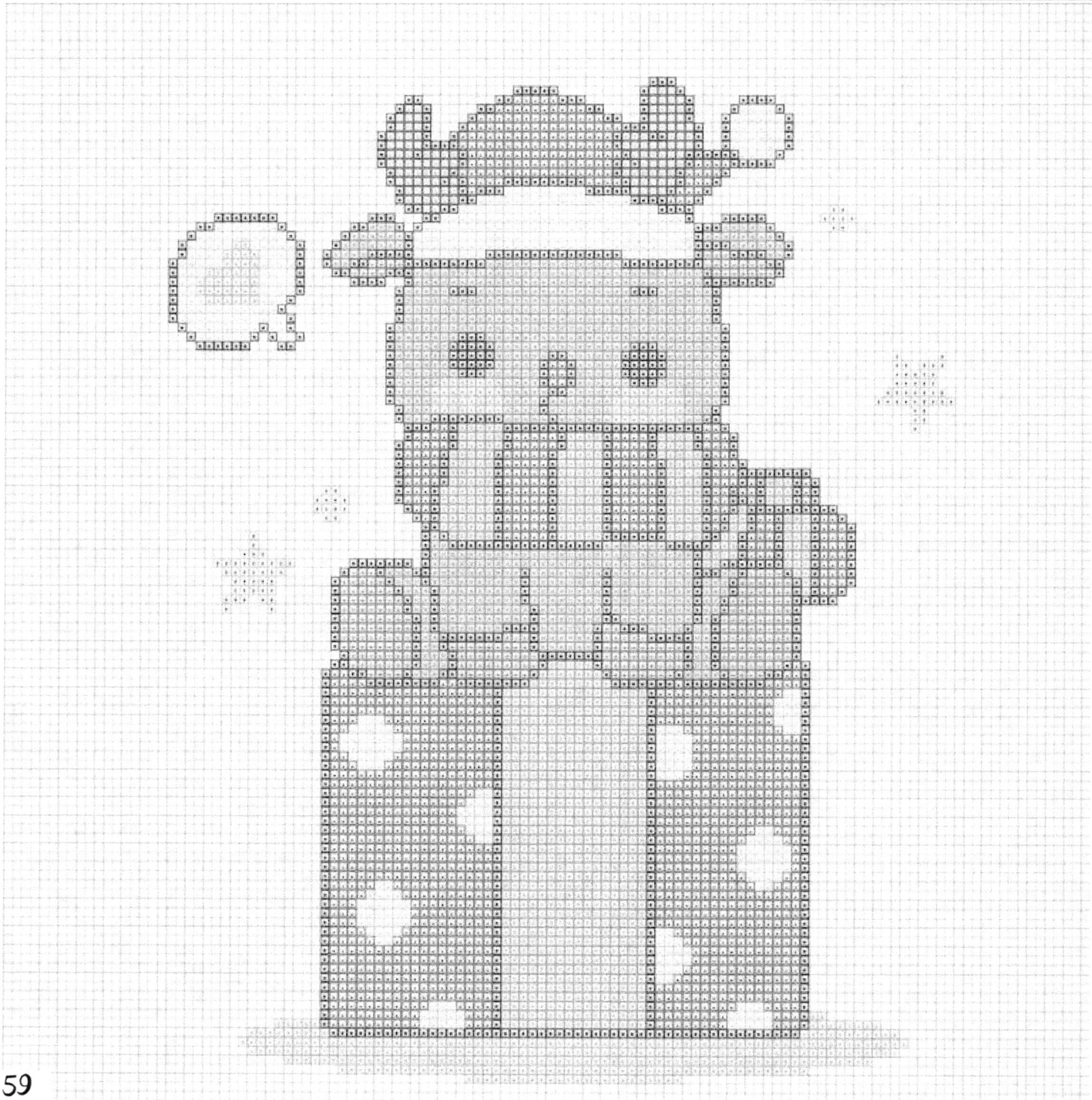

Unicorn with Christmas lights

		Count	Code	Name
★		852	300	Mahogany Vy Dk
⊡		132	3805	Cyclamen Pink
▲		98	973	Canary Bright
⌘		476	3608	Plum Very Light
✛		813	964	Sea Green Light
✖		258	445	Lemon Light
☰		430	605	Cranberry Very Light
◡		2238	White	White

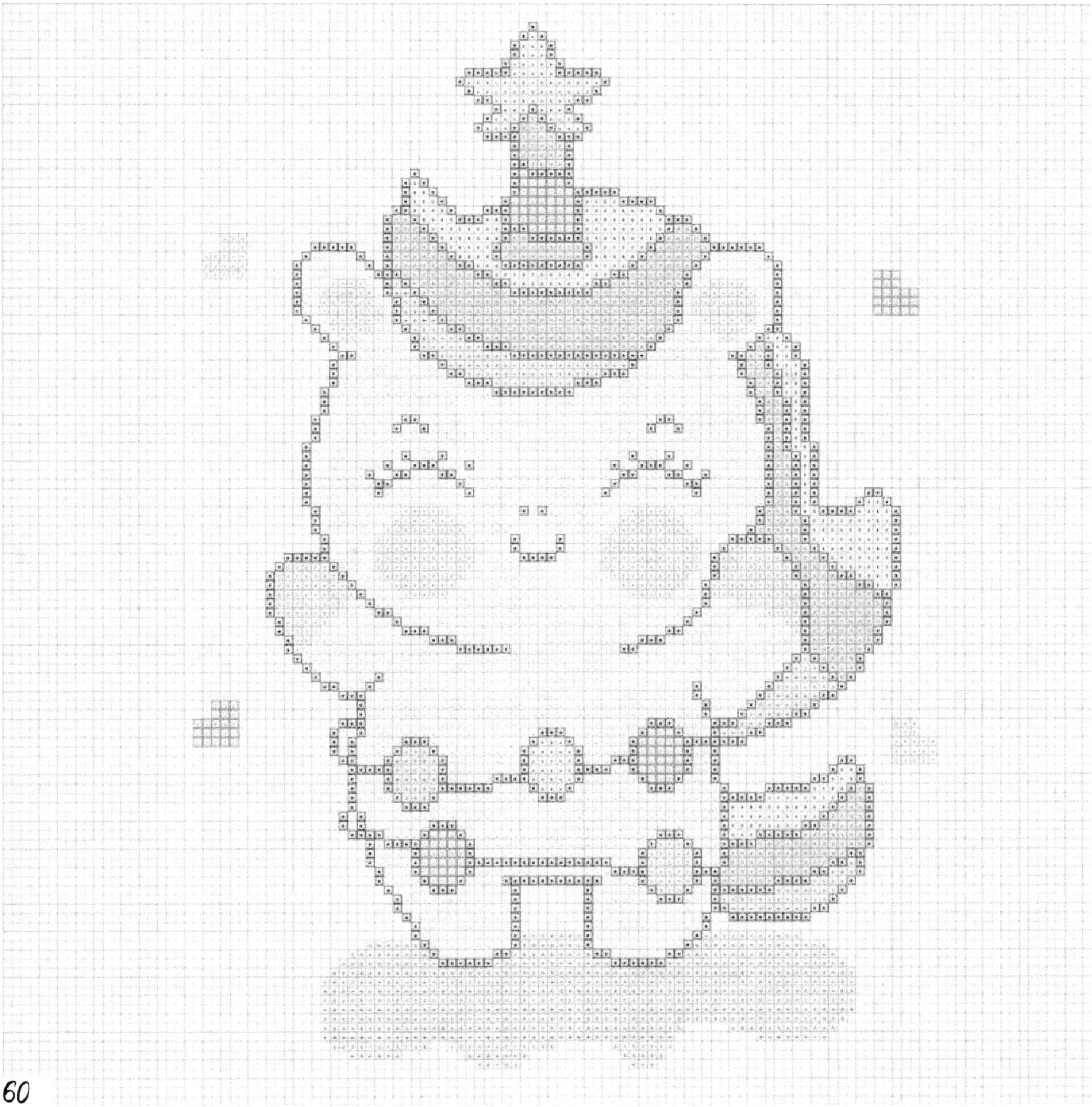

Santa Claus girl

		Count	Code	Name
★		1032	938	Coffee Brown Ult Dk
⊡		272	433	Brown Med
▲		1030	666	Bright Red
✛		113	703	Chartreuse
⌘		1503	307	Lemon
▤		271	3761	Sky Blue Light
✗		100	957	Geranium Pale
⊗		590	739	Tan Ult Vy Lt
⌣		408	White	White

Girl flying with a reindeer balloon

		Count	Code	Name
★		818	898	Coffee Brown Vy Dk
▫		984	632	Desert Sand Ult Vy Dk
▲		141	912	Emerald Green Lt
╀		332	350	Coral Medium
▤		894	603	Cranberry
⌘		670	745	Yellow Pale Light
⚎		444	3770	Tawny Vy Light
⌣		99	White	White

lovely unicorn in a cup

		Count	Code	Name
★	■	583	310	Black
⊡		211	335	Rose
▲		482	893	Carnation Light
+		1587	760	Salmon
◆		363	3689	Mauve Light
≡		494	945	Tawny
✕		704	3770	Tawny Vy Light
◡		828	White	White

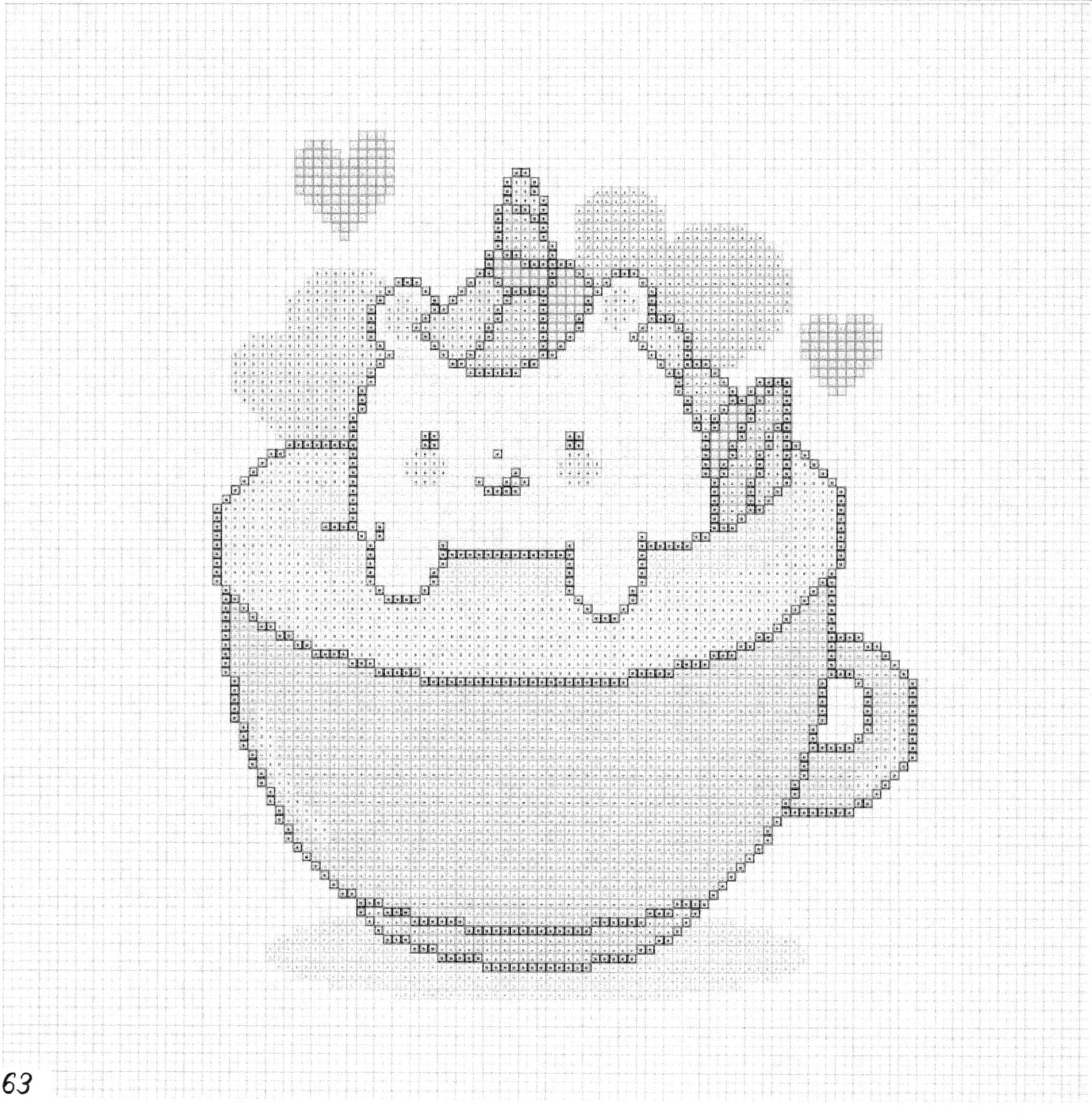

Snowman

		Count	Code	Name
★		290	3838	Lavender Blue Dark
⊡		156	3731	Dusty Rose Very Dark
▲		505	334	Baby Blue Medium
+		437	604	Cranberry Light
⌘		699	3811	Turquoise Very Light
∪		1257	White	White

Bear holding a Christmas tree

		Count	Code	Name
★		1213	898	Coffee Brown Vy Dk
⊡		416	335	Rose
▲		1056	992	Aquamarine Lt
⊠		2956	3854	Autumn Gold Med
⊞		201	307	Lemon
☰		779	738	Tan Very Light
⺕		447	3326	Rose Light
⌘		223	3609	Plum Ultra Light
⌣		75	White	White

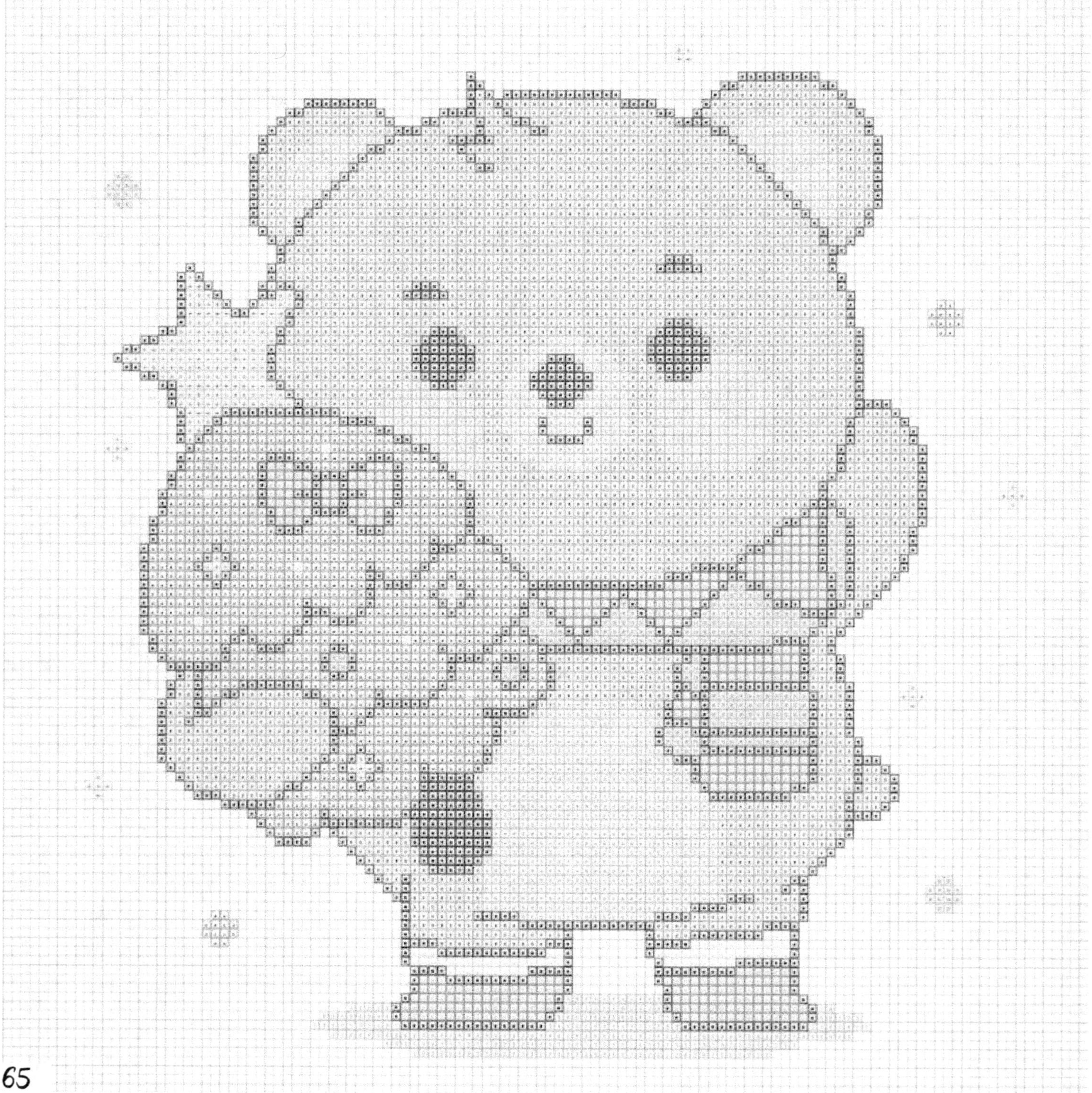

Tigger at Christmas

		Count	Code	Name
★		801	938	Coffee Brown Ult Dk
⊡		25	911	Emerald Green Med
▲		1842	666	Bright Red
+		1255	725	Topaz Med Lt
≣		220	3608	Plum Very Light
⌘		1235	3708	Melon Light
✗		133	677	Old Gold Vy Lt
⌣		472	White	White

Girl wearing a Christmas tree costume

	Count	Code	Name
★	619	898	Coffee Brown Vy Dk
□	225	610	Drab Brown Dk
▲	109	666	Bright Red
✿	1457	703	Chartreuse
✕	138	725	Topaz Med Lt
≡	50	893	Carnation Light
╋	157	341	Blue Violet Light
∈	234	819	Baby Pink Light
⊞	18	White	White

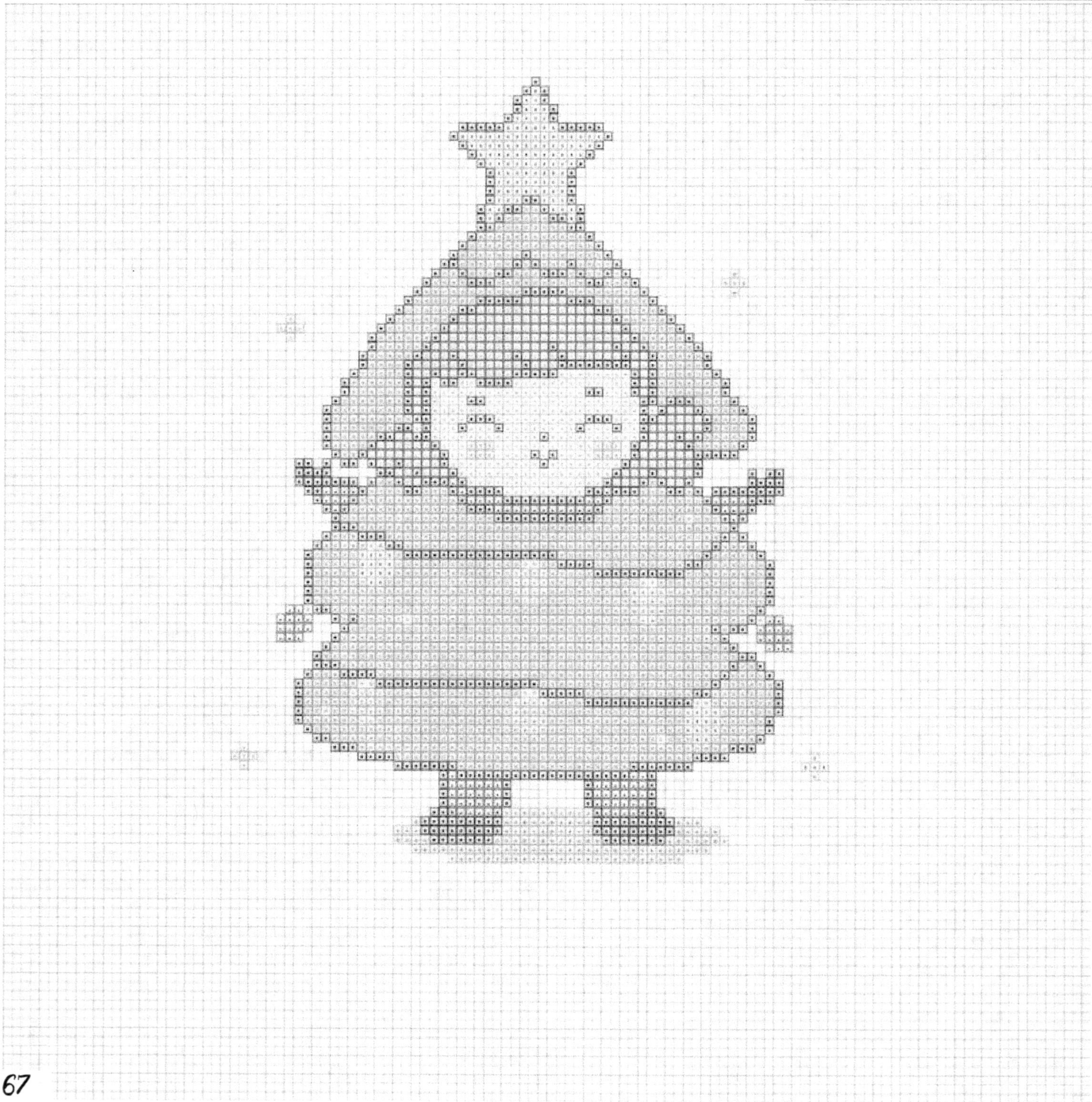

Magician girl with a heart wand

		Count	Code	Name
★	■	898	327	Violet Dark
⊡		774	156	Blue Violet Med Lt
▲		454	3608	Plum Very Light
⊞		379	603	Cranberry
⊠		239	964	Sea Green Light
≣		300	445	Lemon Light
⌘		218	3708	Melon Light
⌣		705	712	Cream

Valentine gnome

		Count	Code	Name
★	■	685	310	Black
▫		1253	899	Rose Medium
▲		896	3609	Plum Ultra Light
✚		115	165	Moss Green Vy Lt
☰		476	605	Cranberry Very Light
⌘		647	3713	Salmon Very Light
⌣		869	White	White

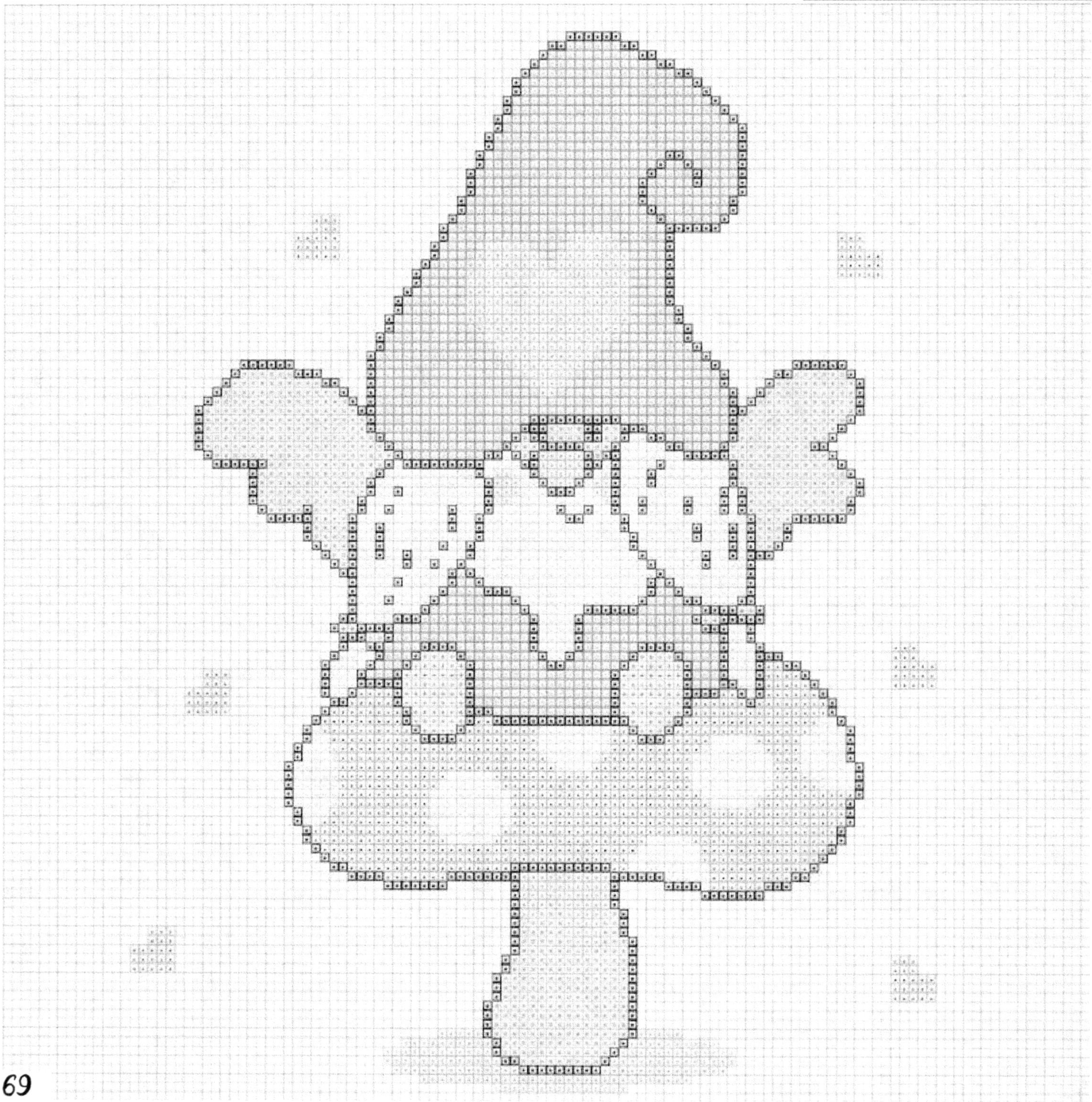

Cupid with heart arrows

		Count	Code	Name
★		1030	814	Garnet Dark
⊡		374	891	Carnation Dark
▲		111	899	Rose Medium
⌘		331	341	Blue Violet Light
◈		354	3609	Plum Ultra Light
≣		666	605	Cranberry Very Light
⊗		3160	828	Sky Blue Vy Lt
＋		233	727	Topaz Vy Lt
⌣		2494	White	White

Happy unicorn holding a heart balloon

		Count	Code	Name
★		806	898	Coffee Brown Vy Dk
⬚		773	3609	Plum Ultra Light
▲		971	828	Sky Blue Vy Lt
＋		258	727	Topaz Vy Lt
≡		1090	963	Dusty Rose Ult Vy Lt
∪		1926	White	White

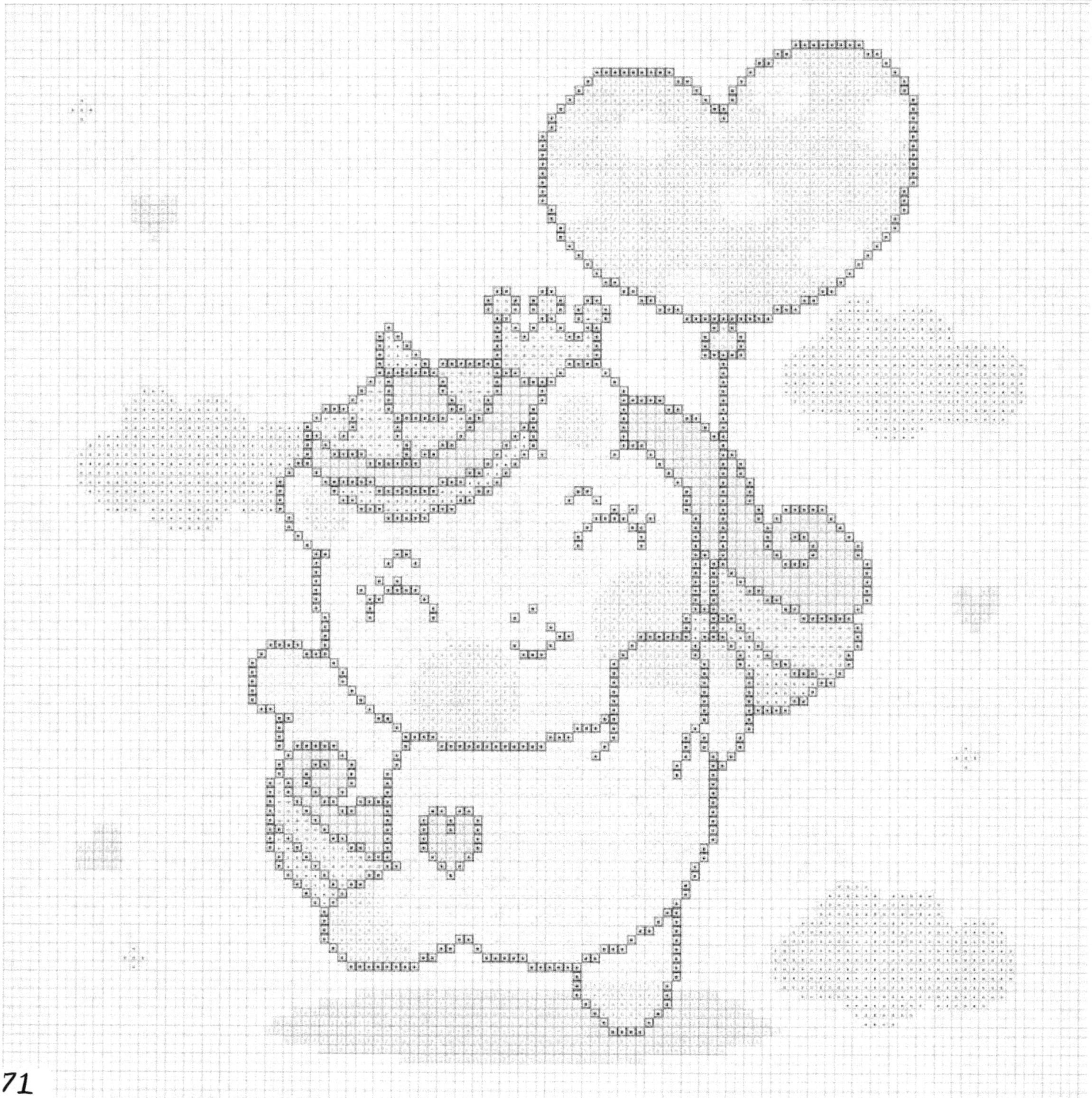

Happy unicorn with the gifts

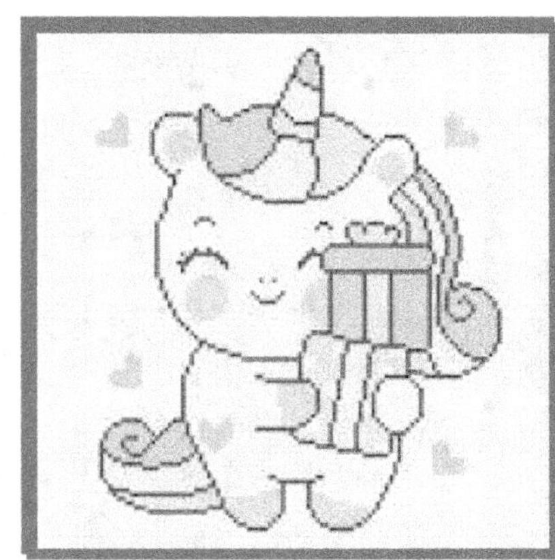

	Count	Code	Name
★	1030	898	Coffee Brown Vy Dk
▫	1152	3609	Plum Ultra Light
▲	466	605	Cranberry Very Light
+	671	828	Sky Blue Vy Lt
≡	631	727	Topaz Vy Lt
◡	2410	White	White

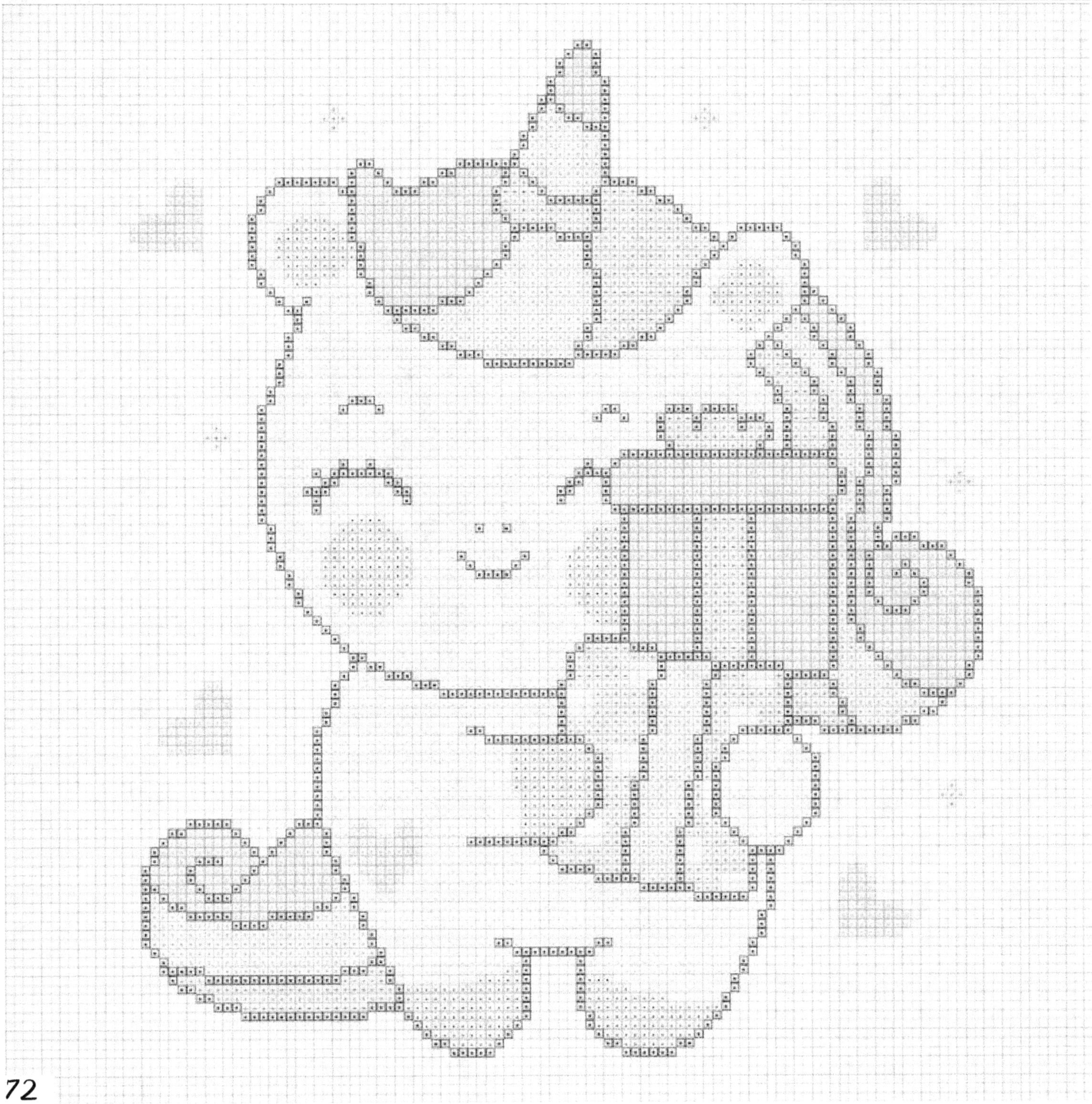

Valentine bunnies

		Count	Code	Name
★	■	326	500	Blue Green Vy Dk
⊡	■	331	3685	Mauve Very Dark
▲	▨	8	581	Moss Green
△	▨	161	519	Sky Blue
⊞	☐	34	307	Lemon
⌘	▨	821	604	Cranberry Light
⊠	▨	265	415	Pearl Gray
☰	☐	1092	828	Sky Blue Vy Lt
⊗	☐	1118	3713	Salmon Very Light

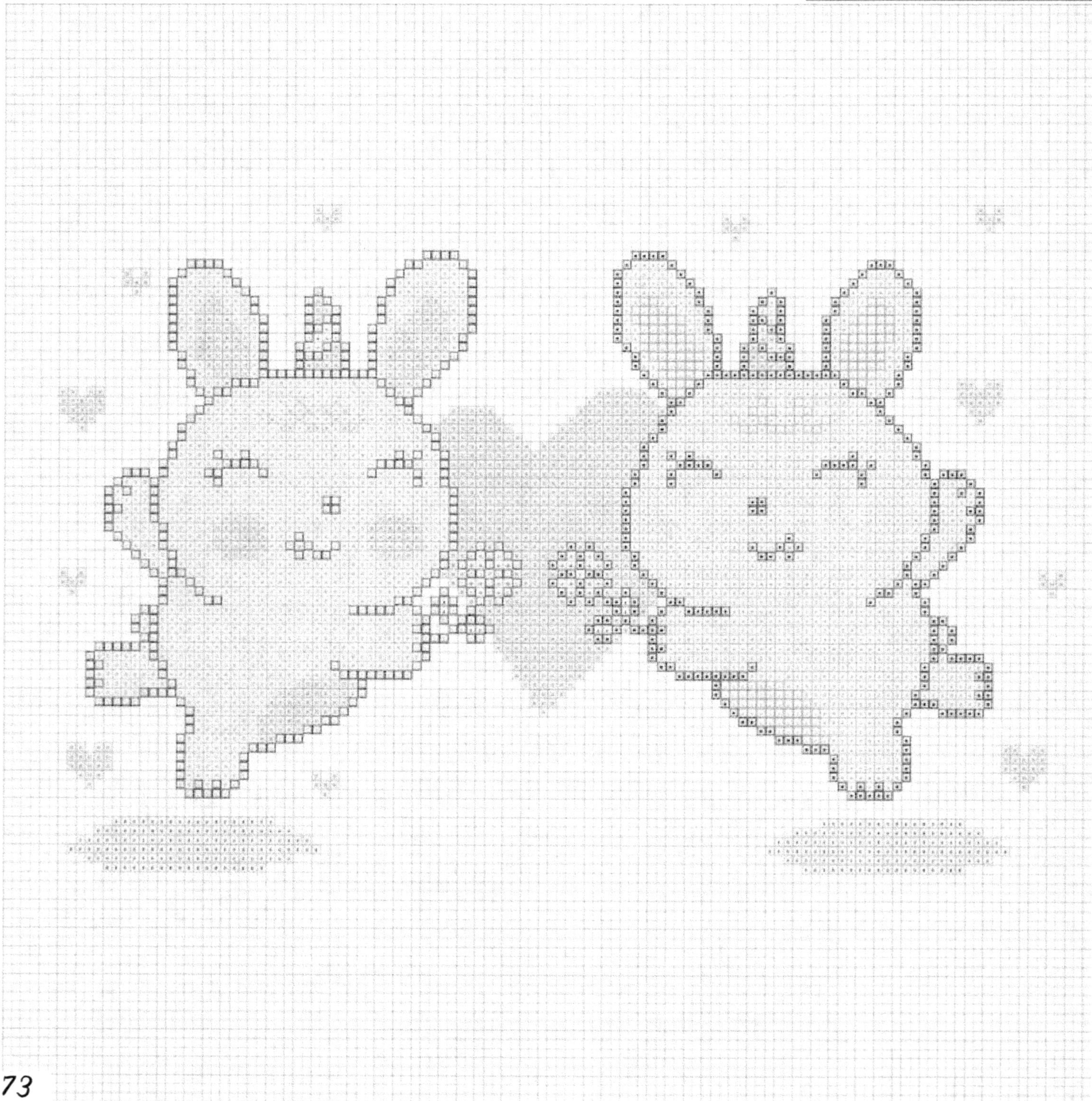

love in the air

	Count	Code	Name
★	1008	154	Grape Very Dark
▢	377	347	Salmon Very Dark
▲	1937	350	Coral Medium
＋	162	972	Canary Deep
≡	294	747	Peacock Blue Vy Lt
∪	767	White	White

Cute toilet friends

		Count	Code	Name
★		132	938	Coffee Brown Ult Dk
⊡		1315	801	Coffee Brown Dk
▲		311	976	Golden Brown Med
⊞		432	351	Coral
⌘		74	503	Blue Green Med
✕		1306	3853	Autumn Gold Dk
▤		393	3825	Pumpkin Pale
⌐		63	603	Cranberry
⊗		294	928	Gray Green Vy Lt
‿		2058	White	White

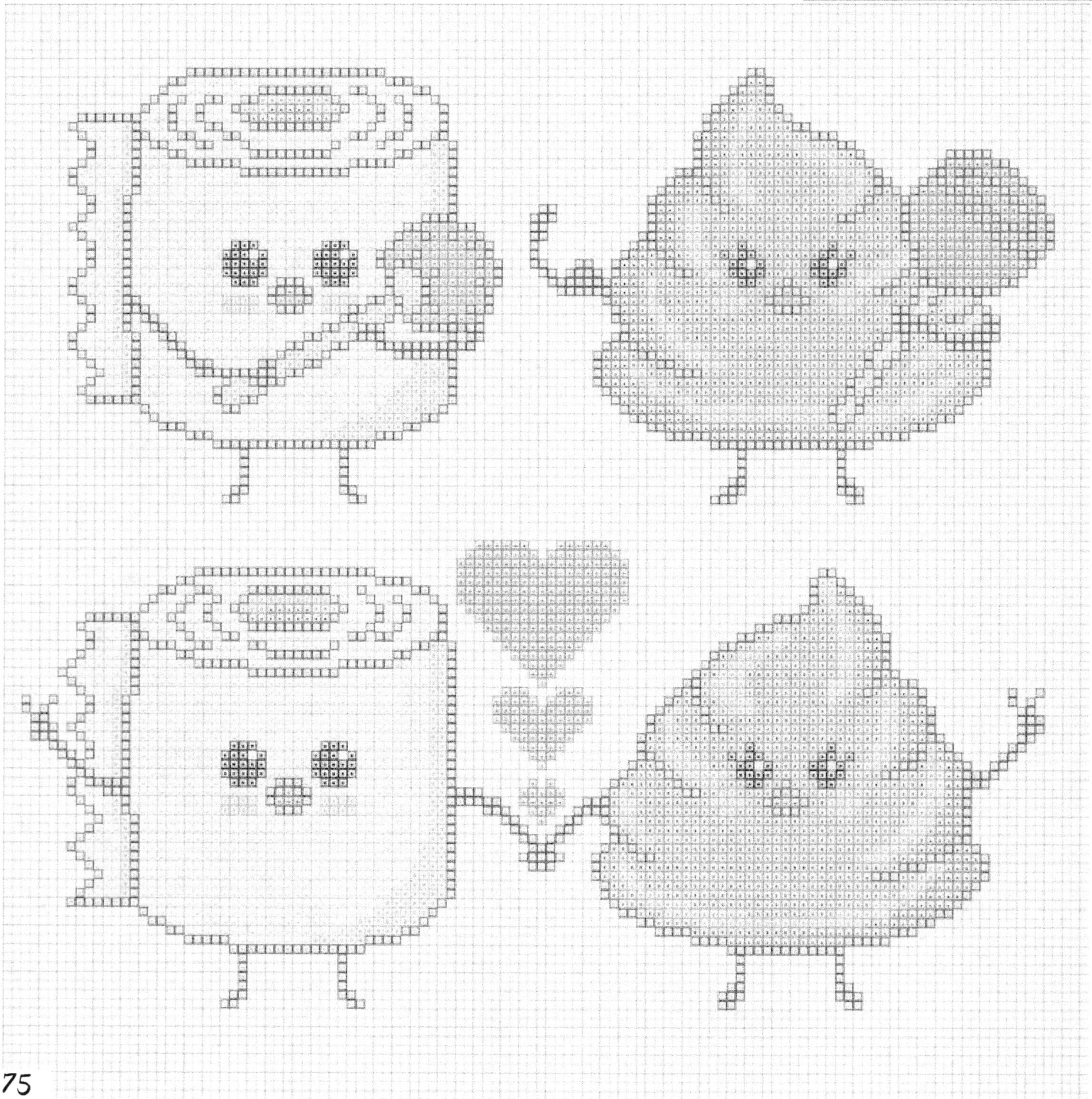

Game console gift

		Count	Code	Name
★		1312	208	Lavender Very Dark
⊡		136	472	Avocado Grn U Lt
▲		1236	157	Cornflower Blue Vy Lt
+		348	3609	Plum Ultra Light
≡		510	3841	Baby Blue Pale
⊗		1138	677	Old Gold Vy Lt
‿		1249	762	Pearl Gray Vy Lt

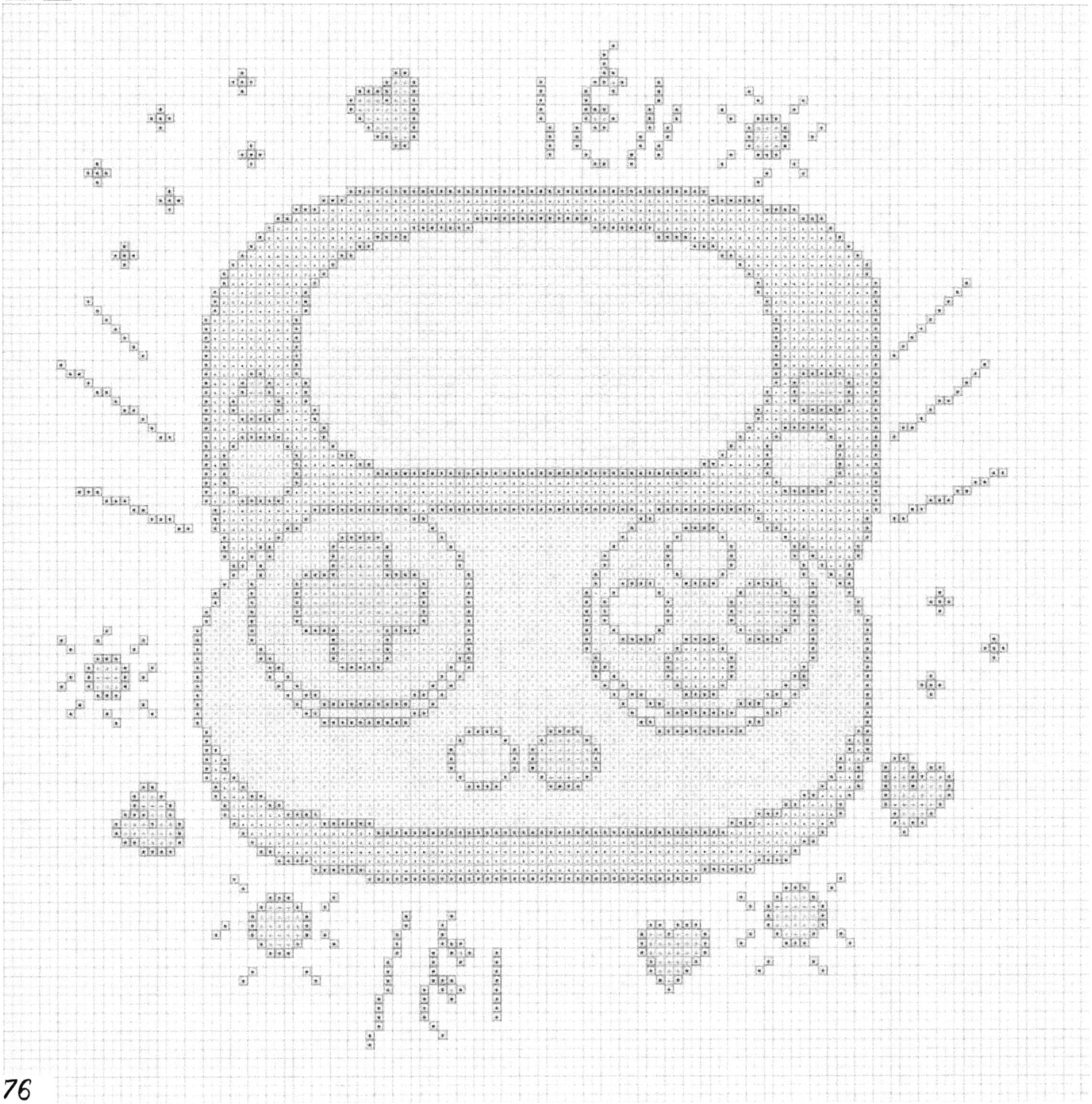

Dracula cat

		Count	Code	Name
★		986	154	Grape Very Dark
⊡		1775	552	Violet Medium
▲		833	169	Pewter Light
⊞		73	721	Orange Spice Med
≡		114	741	Tangerine Med
⊠		104	743	Yellow Med
⌘		219	3609	Plum Ultra Light
⌣		784	White	White

Ghost with a cupcake and candies

		Count	Code	Name
★		851	550	Violet Very Dark
⊡		705	704	Chartreuse Bright
▲		923	209	Lavender Dark
+		499	947	Burnt Orange
▤		127	444	Lemon Dark
⊗		1150	3716	Dusty Rose Med Vy Lt
⌘		488	967	Apricot Very Light
⌣		829	White	White

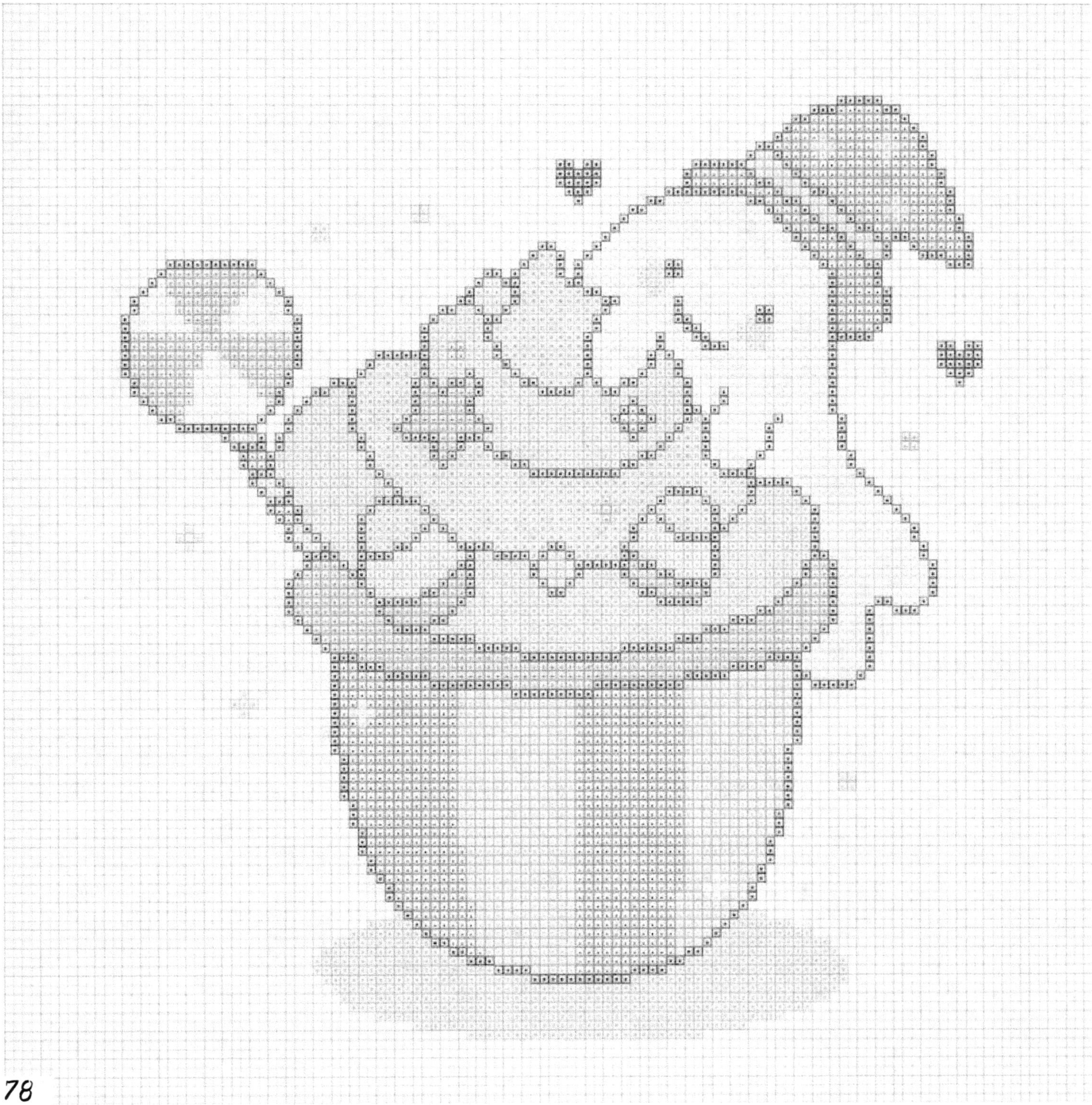

Cat with a magic pot cauldron

		Count	Code	Name
★		1300	154	Grape Very Dark
⊡		1823	552	Violet Medium
▲		1724	646	Beaver Gray Dk
⊠		226	166	Moss Green Md Lt
☰		157	741	Tangerine Med
⌘		147	3806	Cyclamen Pink Light

Witch girl

		Count	Code	Name
★		781	310	Black
⬚		1568	844	Beaver Gray Ult Dk
▲		29	433	Brown Med
+		67	946	Burnt Orange Med
✕		237	3835	Grape Medium
☰		163	704	Chartreuse Bright
⌘		982	603	Cranberry
⌣		598	819	Baby Pink Light

Funny trick or treat girl

		Count	Code	Name
★		1356	310	Black
▫		501	3803	Mauve Dark
▲		174	209	Lavender Dark
≣		790	3805	Cyclamen Pink
⊼		1550	947	Burnt Orange
⌘		36	444	Lemon Dark
⊗		104	957	Geranium Pale
┼		525	3713	Salmon Very Light

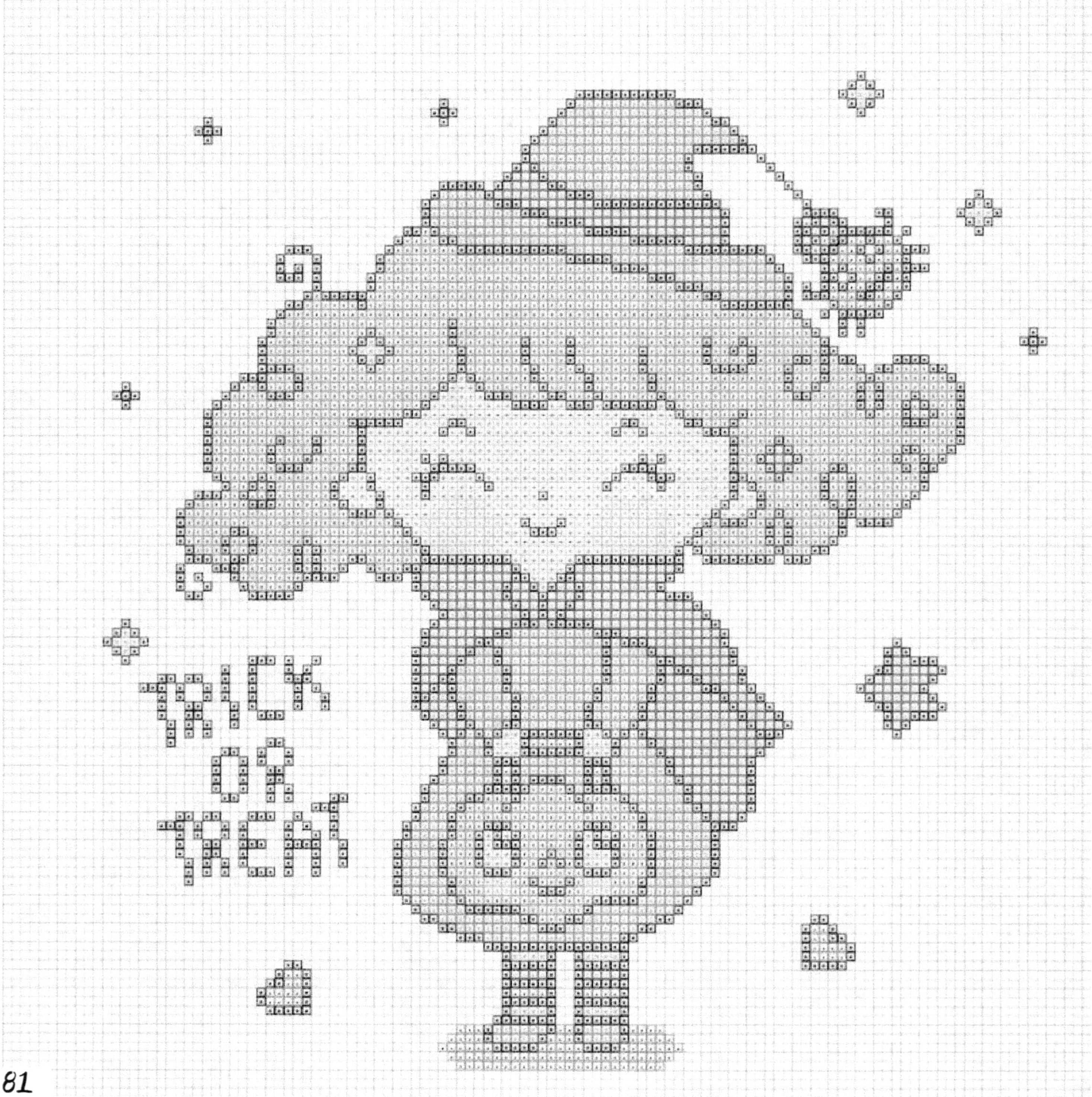

Floral unicorn

	Count	Code	Name
★	66	300	Mahogany Vy Dk
▣	67	562	Jade Medium
▲	282	3835	Grape Medium
⌧	190	209	Lavender Dark
▶	76	166	Moss Green Md Lt
⌘	98	899	Rose Medium
◆	216	993	Aquamarine Vy Lt
▤	162	402	Mahogany Vy Lt
⊞	573	603	Cranberry
⊘	84	211	Lavender Light
⌣	1458	739	Tan Ult Vy Lt

Halloween party girl

	Count	Code	Name
★	893	154	Grape Very Dark
▢	159	946	Burnt Orange Med
▲	748	3835	Grape Medium
≣	95	704	Chartreuse Bright
⊞	863	972	Canary Deep
⊗	547	603	Cranberry
⌘	227	168	Pewter Very Light
⌣	354	819	Baby Pink Light

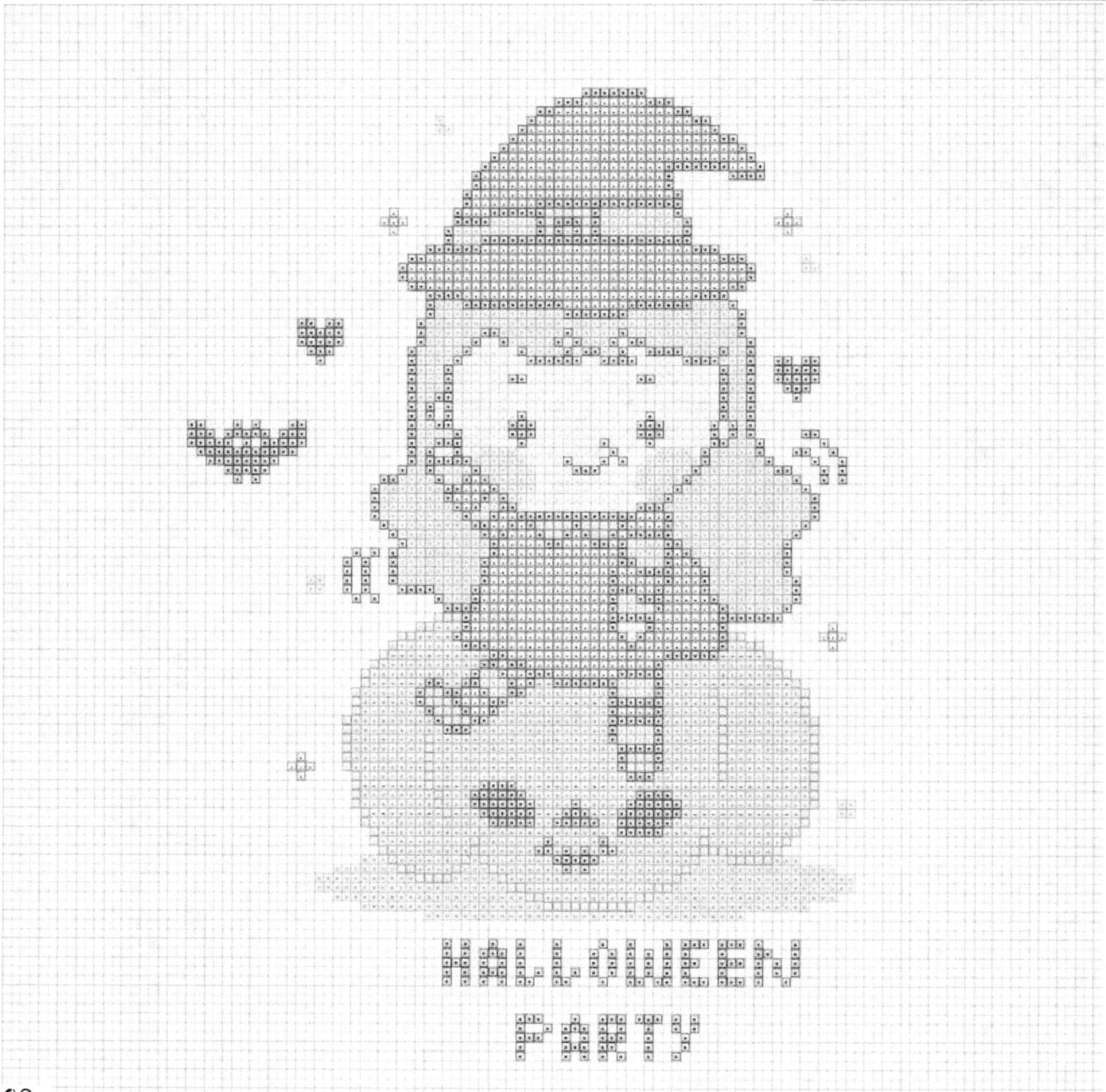

Girl holding a pumpkin bucket

		Count	Code	Name
★		1464	938	Coffee Brown Ult Dk
▢		724	433	Brown Med
▲		322	740	Tangerine
⊥		23	704	Chartreuse Bright
☰		494	209	Lavender Dark
⌘		102	603	Cranberry
⌣		546	819	Baby Pink Light

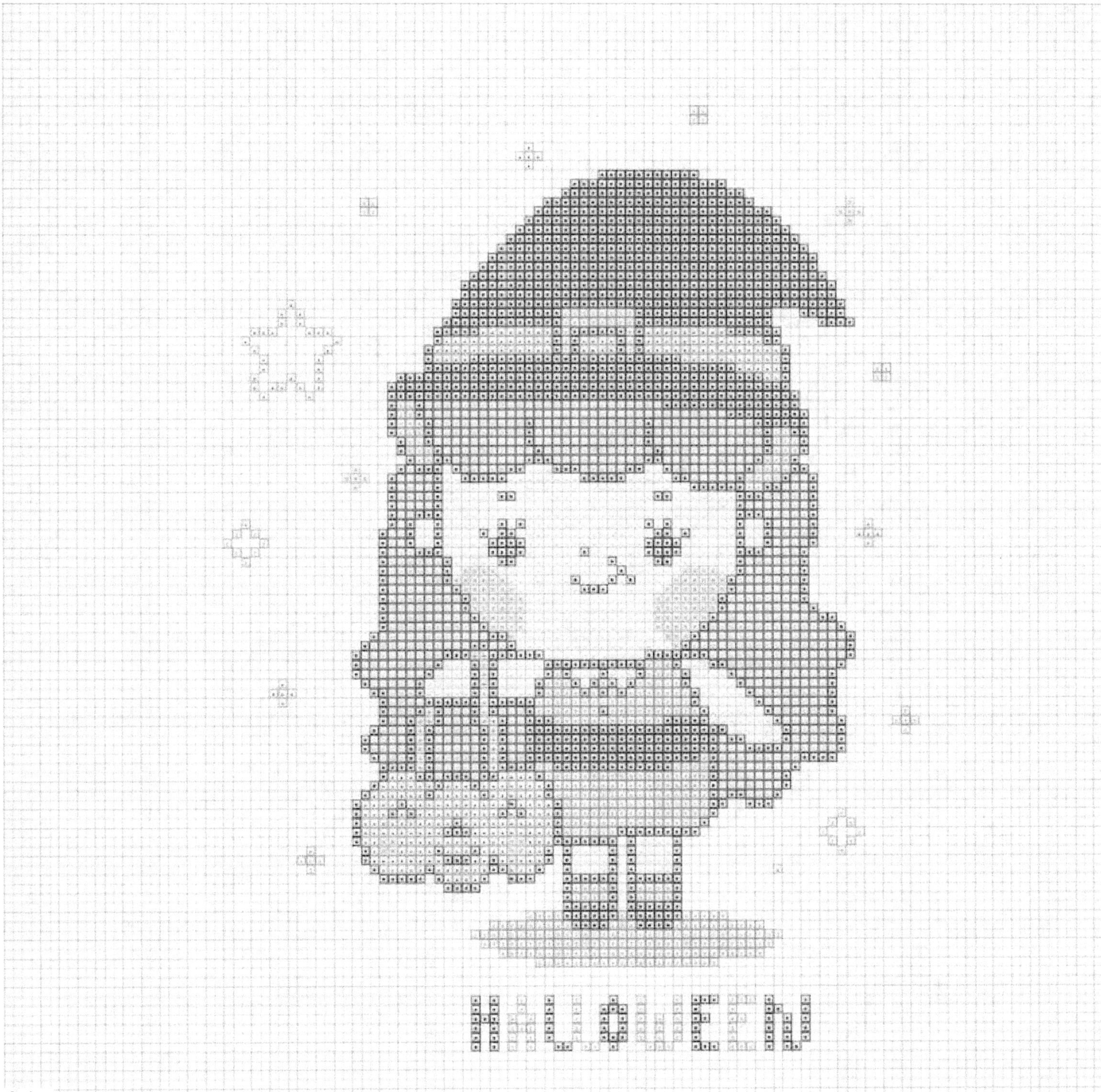

Witch with a big pumpkin

		Count	Code	Name
★	■	954	310	Black
⊡		1185	3837	Lavender Ultra Dark
▲		267	704	Chartreuse Bright
≡		1080	972	Canary Deep
⊞		562	603	Cranberry
⌘		671	168	Pewter Very Light
✶		127	605	Cranberry Very Light
∪		418	819	Baby Pink Light

Zombie

		Count	Code	Name
★		1412	939	Navy Blue Very Dark
⊡		1007	158	Cornflower Blu M V D
▲		120	943	Green Bright Md
+		1162	954	Nile Green
▤		88	3806	Cyclamen Pink Light
◡		25	White	White

Witch on a broom

	Count	Code	Name
★	1267	550	Violet Very Dark
⊡	772	208	Lavender Very Dark
▲	134	646	Beaver Gray Dk
⊠	190	704	Chartreuse Bright
≣	927	741	Tangerine Med
⊕	1059	3609	Plum Ultra Light
∪	486	712	Cream

Fast food

	Count	Code	Name
★	1194	898	Coffee Brown Vy Dk
⊡	74	3777	Terra Cotta Vy Dk
▲	612	350	Coral Medium
⊞	196	703	Chartreuse
⌘	1859	3853	Autumn Gold Dk
⚎	806	726	Topaz Light
⊗	421	3766	Peacock Blue Light
☰	116	3856	Mahogany Ult Vy Lt
⌣	77	White	White

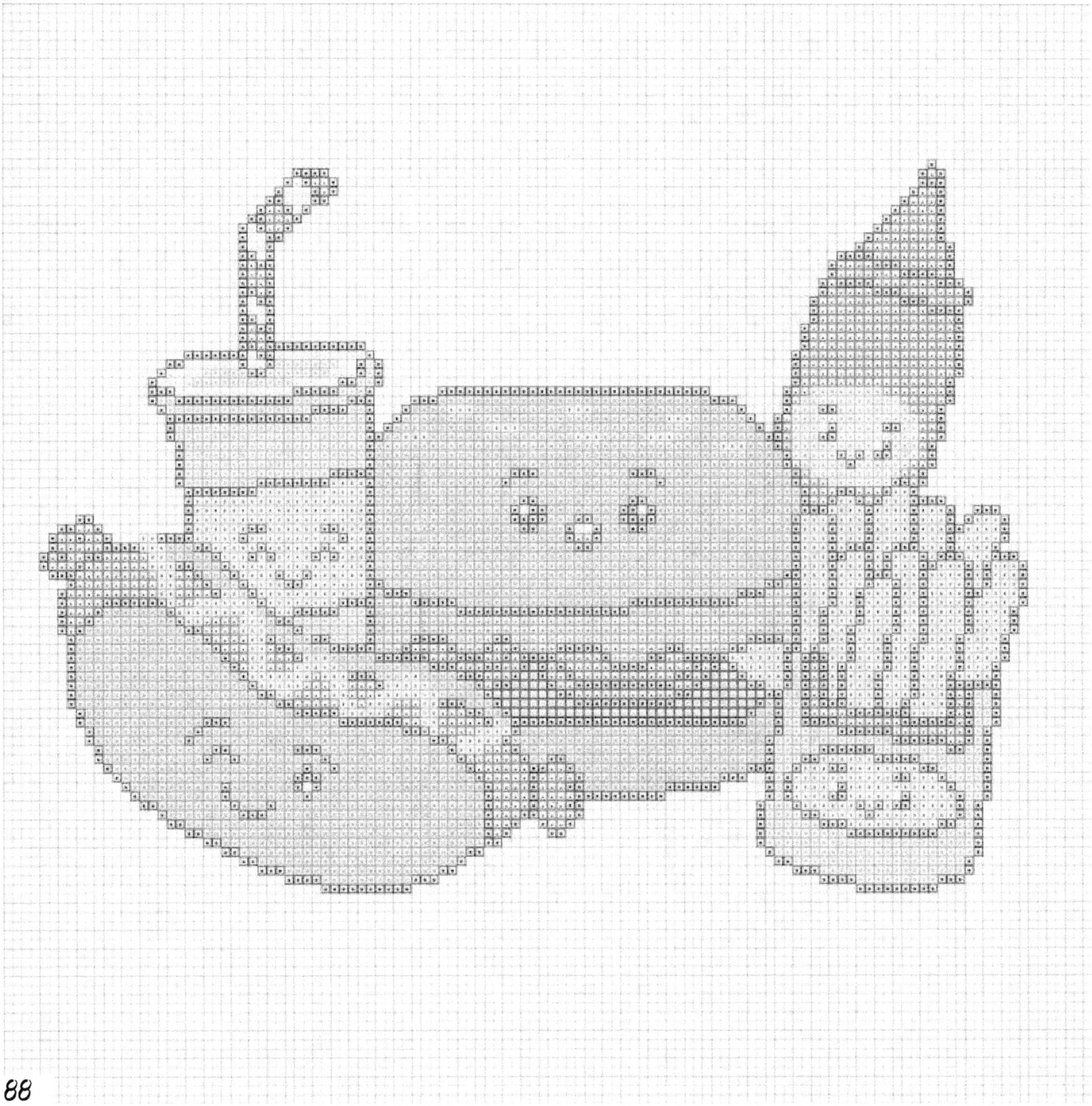

Taco

		Count	Code	Name
★		705	898	Coffee Brown Vy Dk
⊡		152	912	Emerald Green Lt
▲		240	321	Red
⊞		241	350	Coral Medium
⊻		237	703	Chartreuse
⊗		873	972	Canary Deep
▤		1887	726	Topaz Light
⌘		349	3078	Golden Yellow Vy Lt
⌣		8	White	White

Bread and omelet

		Count	Code	Name
★		653	632	Desert Sand Ult Vy Dk
⊟		356	436	Tan
▲		197	3833	Raspberry Light
⊞		467	742	Tangerine Light
⊠		1412	738	Tan Very Light
☰		316	3761	Sky Blue Light
⌣		1772	3866	Mocha Brn Ult Vy Lt

Ramen

		Count	Code	Name
★		1581	814	Garnet Dark
▫		398	782	Topaz Dark
▲		94	471	Avocado Grn V Lt
⊞		239	3833	Raspberry Light
▤		1193	726	Topaz Light
✗		271	3855	Autumn Gold Lt
⌘		1736	3609	Plum Ultra Light
∪		171	White	White

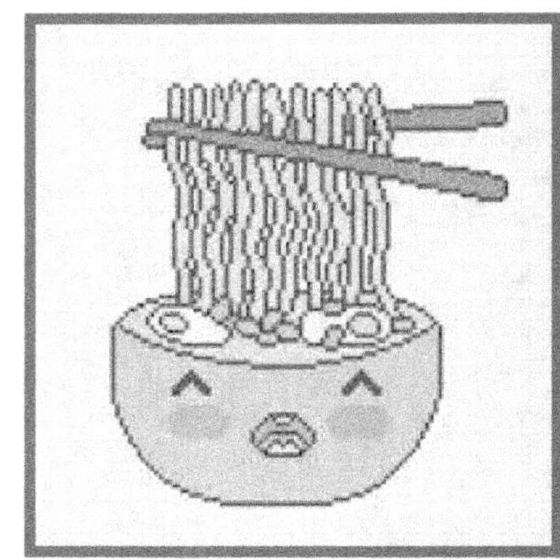

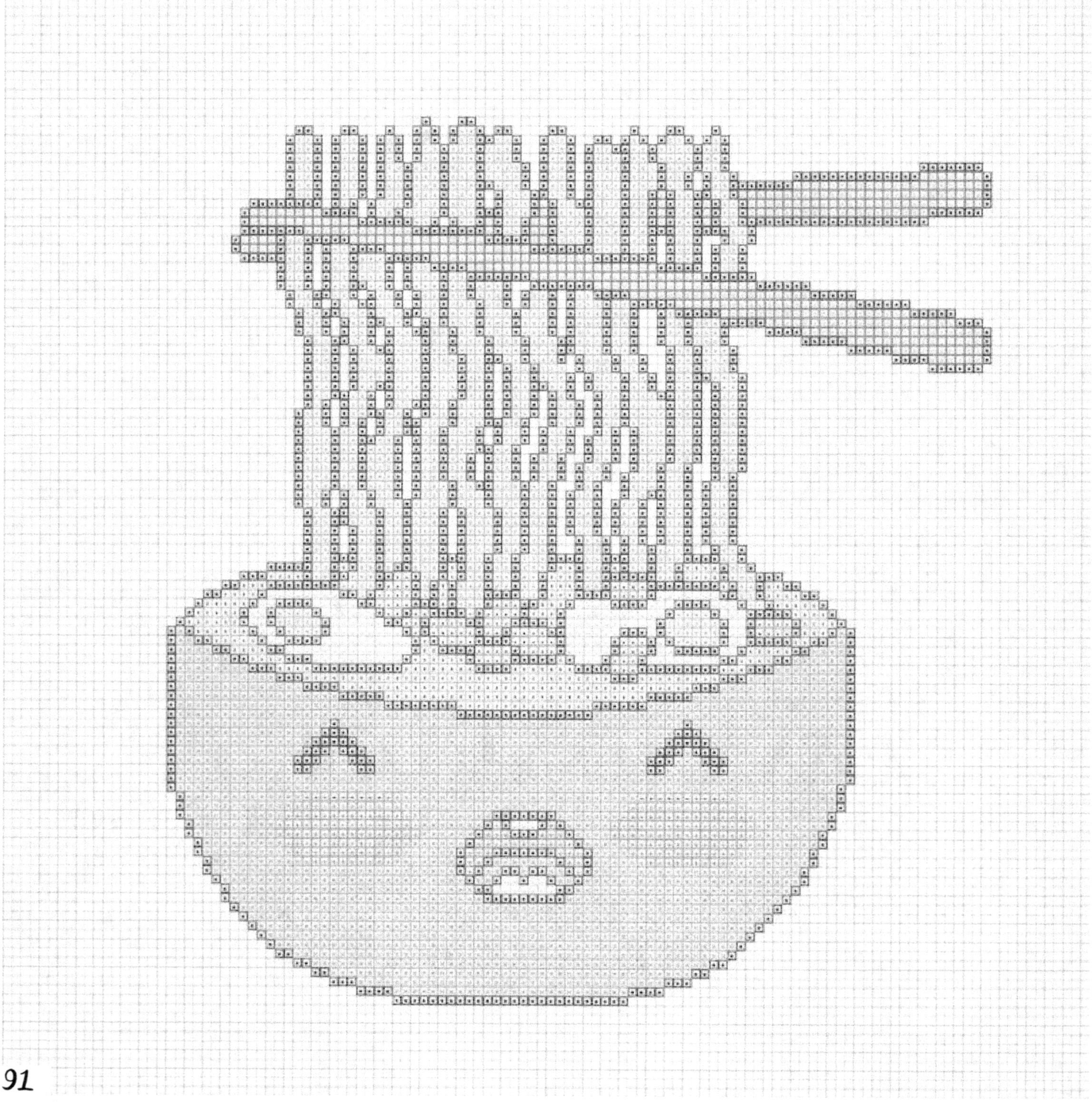

Avocado in love

		Count	Code	Name
★		582	3371	Black Brown
□		132	433	Brown Med
▲		423	911	Emerald Green Med
▤		72	666	Bright Red
✗		1832	470	Avocado Grn Lt
⊞		24	352	Coral Light

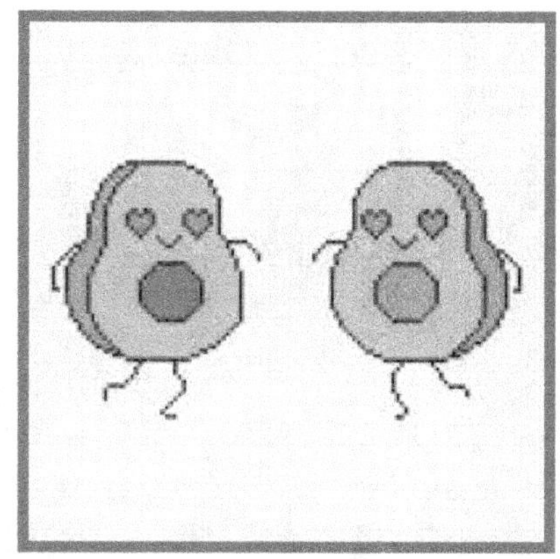

Burger

		Count	Code	Name
★	■	599	310	Black
⊡		287	433	Brown Med
▲		159	905	Parrot Green Dk
⊞		198	347	Salmon Very Dark
⊠		118	606	Orange-Red Bright
⌘		238	703	Chartreuse
▦		872	3776	Mahogany Light
◈		171	444	Lemon Dark
⊗		322	3854	Autumn Gold Med
⊔	☐	8	White	White

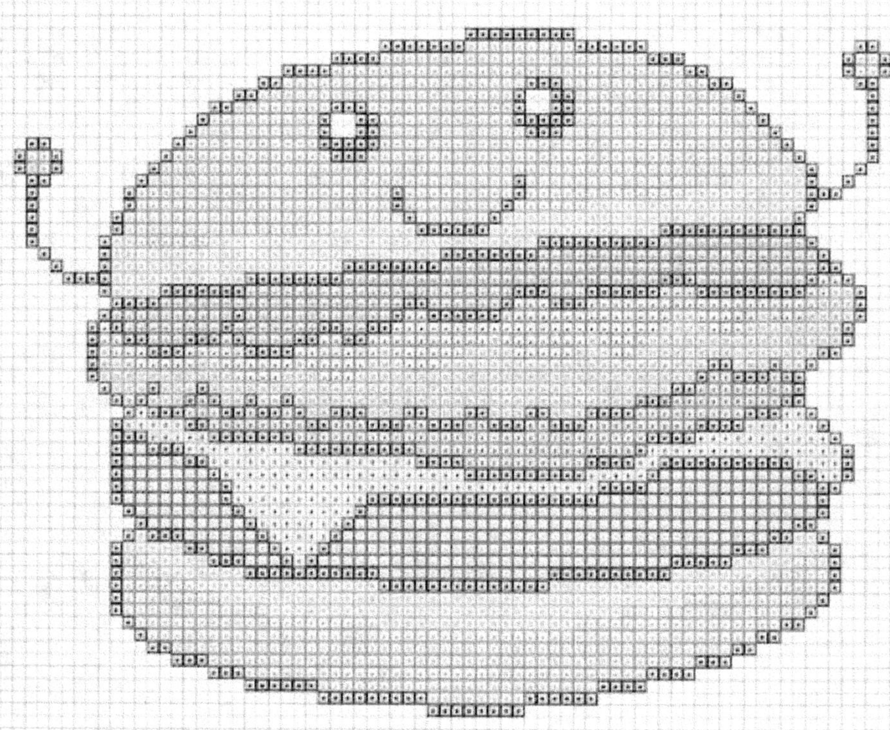

Fried chicken bucket

	Count	Code	Name
★ ■	647	310	Black
☐	610	321	Red
▲	820	3776	Mahogany Light
┼	343	453	Shell Gray Light
⌣ ☐	823	White	White

Sweet macarons with jam

		Count	Code	Name
★		1195	550	Violet Very Dark
⊡		1069	553	Violet
▲		1273	210	Lavender Medium
┼		232	3821	Straw
✿		239	3608	Plum Very Light
≣		623	3811	Turquoise Very Light
◉		519	3708	Melon Light
✕		1339	3713	Salmon Very Light
∪		287	White	White

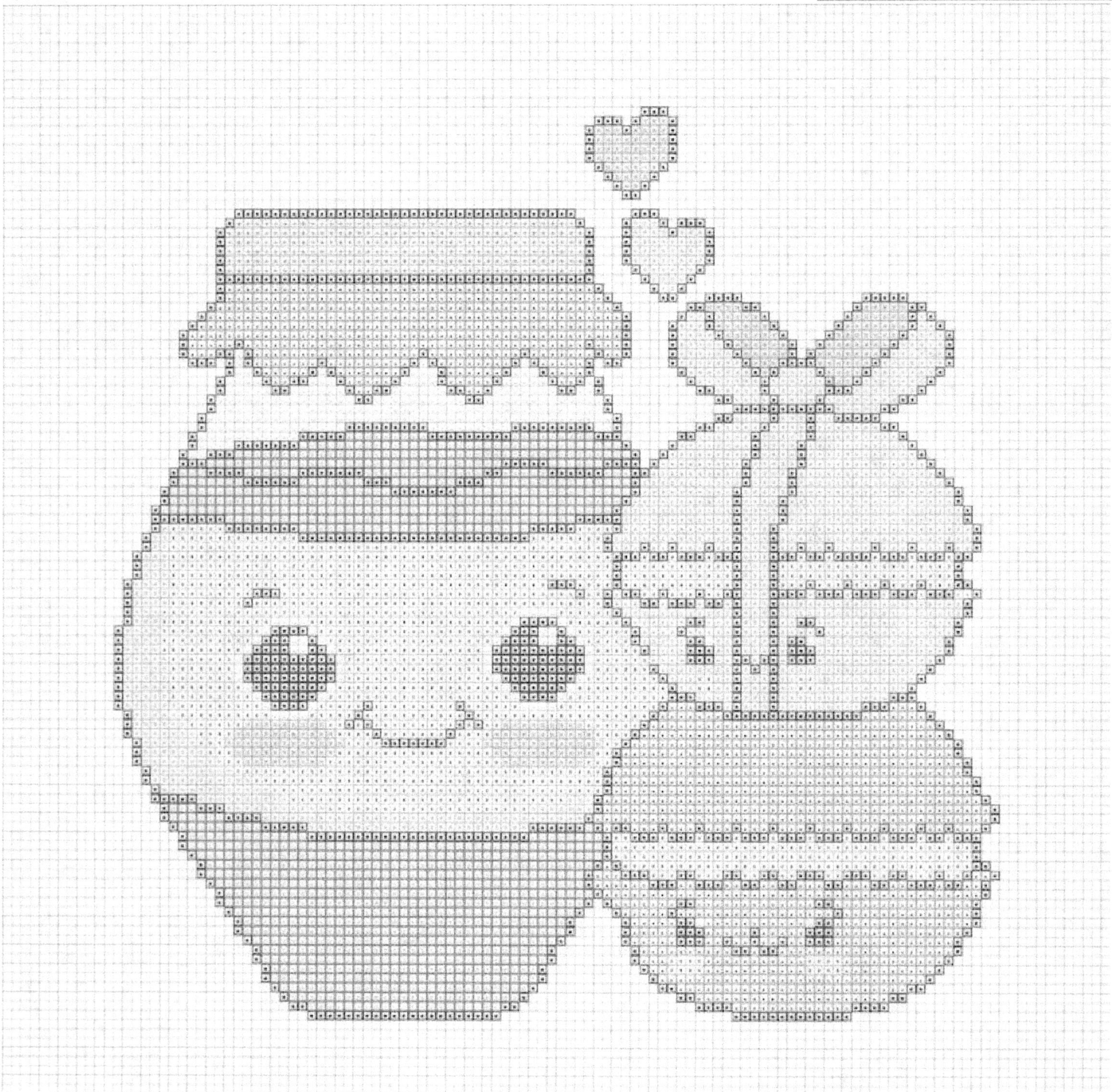

Pizza slice

		Count	Code	Name
★		775	154	Grape Very Dark
▫		118	304	Red Medium
▲		478	921	Copper
⊕		377	666	Bright Red
☰		1047	970	Pumpkin Light
✛		1930	972	Canary Deep
◡		10	White	White

Ice cream bar

		Count	Code	Name
★		544	550	Violet Very Dark
☐		498	3731	Dusty Rose Very Dark
▲		84	3805	Cyclamen Pink
+		280	758	Terra Cotta Vy Lt
☰		2031	3806	Cyclamen Pink Light
⌘		976	745	Yellow Pale Light
⊼		284	3823	Yellow Ultra Pale
⌣		10	White	White

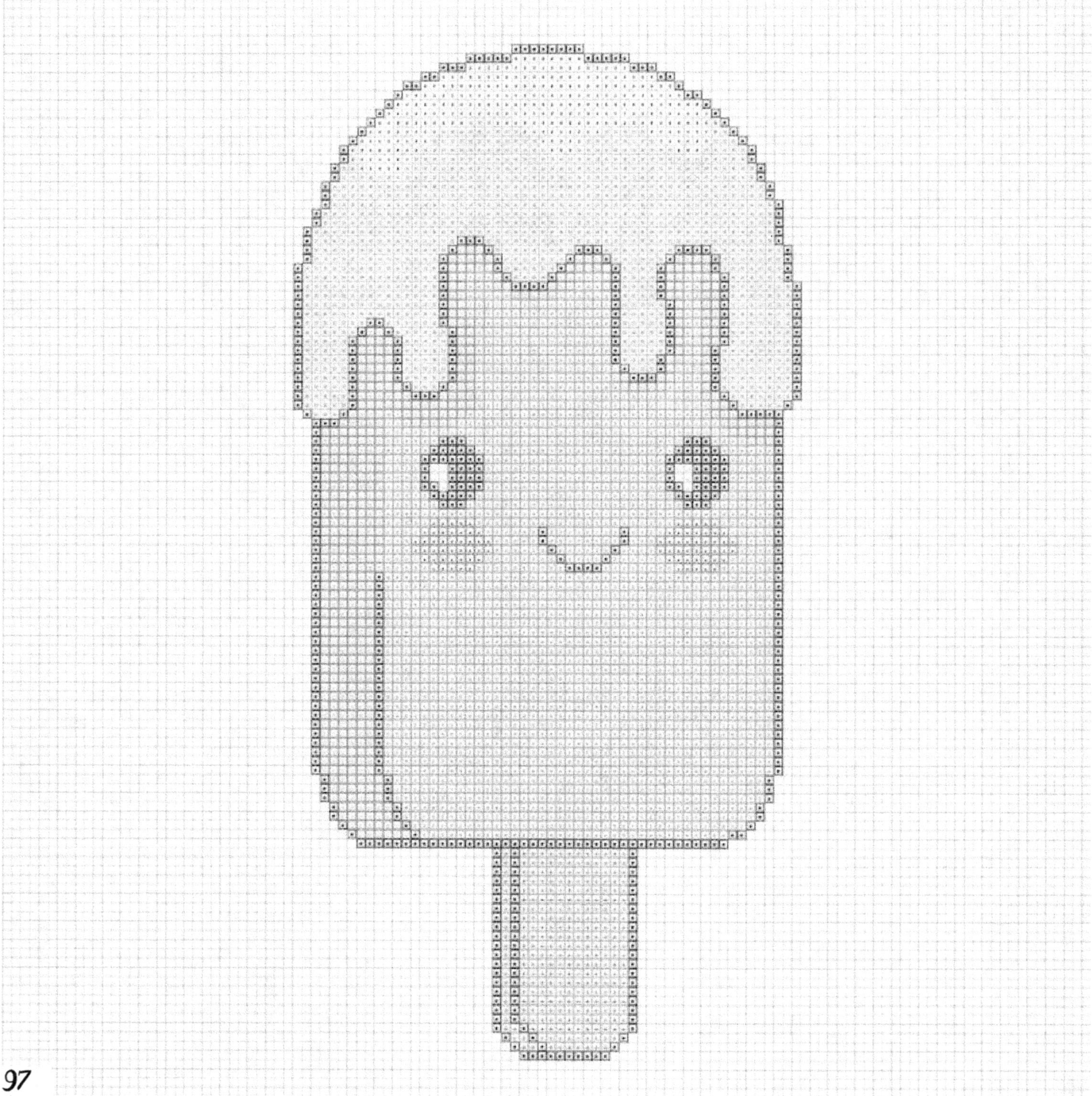

Sushi

		Count	Code	Name
★		837	816	Garnet
⬚		101	351	Coral
▲		243	160	Blue Gray Medium
⊞		506	402	Mahogany Vy Lt
⌘		667	352	Coral Light
⊠		260	3825	Pumpkin Pale
☰		40	165	Moss Green Vy Lt
⊗		534	828	Sky Blue Vy Lt
⌐		567	3713	Salmon Very Light
⌣		1699	White	White

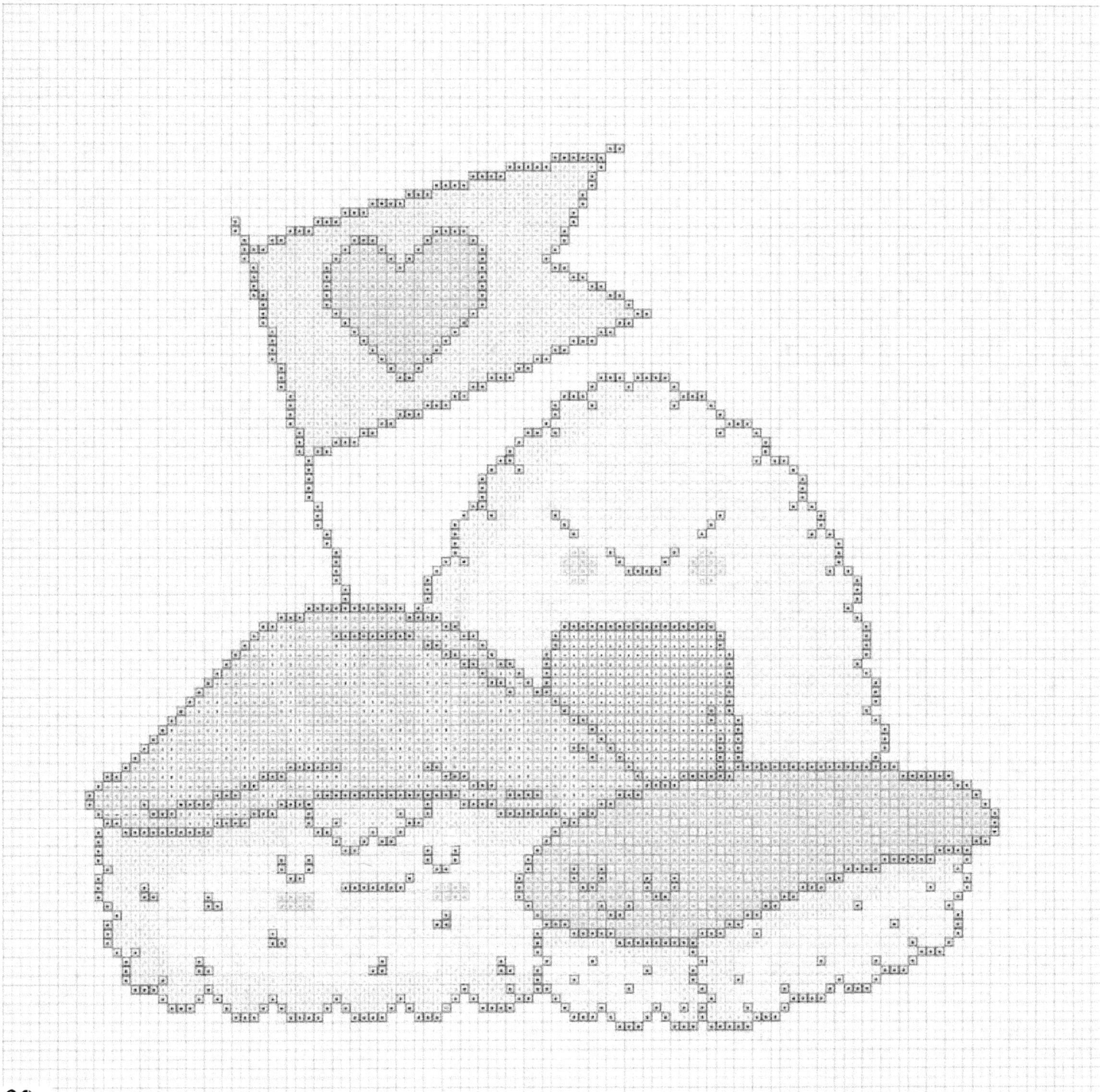

Rice bowl

		Count	Code	Name
★		921	814	Garnet Dark
▫		426	782	Topaz Dark
▲		561	3746	Blue Violet Dark
+		168	3801	Melon Very Dark
⌘		1209	340	Blue Violet Medium
✗		935	3822	Straw Light
▤		292	3708	Melon Light
◡		2054	White	White

Cherry Ice cream

		Count	Code	Name
★		344	550	Violet Very Dark
▫		125	602	Cranberry Medium
▲		1247	209	Lavender Dark
+		388	3778	Terra Cotta Light
≡		592	758	Terra Cotta Vy Lt
⌘		22	603	Cranberry
⌣		2	White	White

Coffee with the cookie

		Count	Code	Name
★		80	791	Cornflower Blue V D
□		329	407	Desert Sand Med
▲		166	3712	Salmon Medium
⊞		1094	437	Tan Light
≡		1258	761	Salmon Light
∪		8	White	White

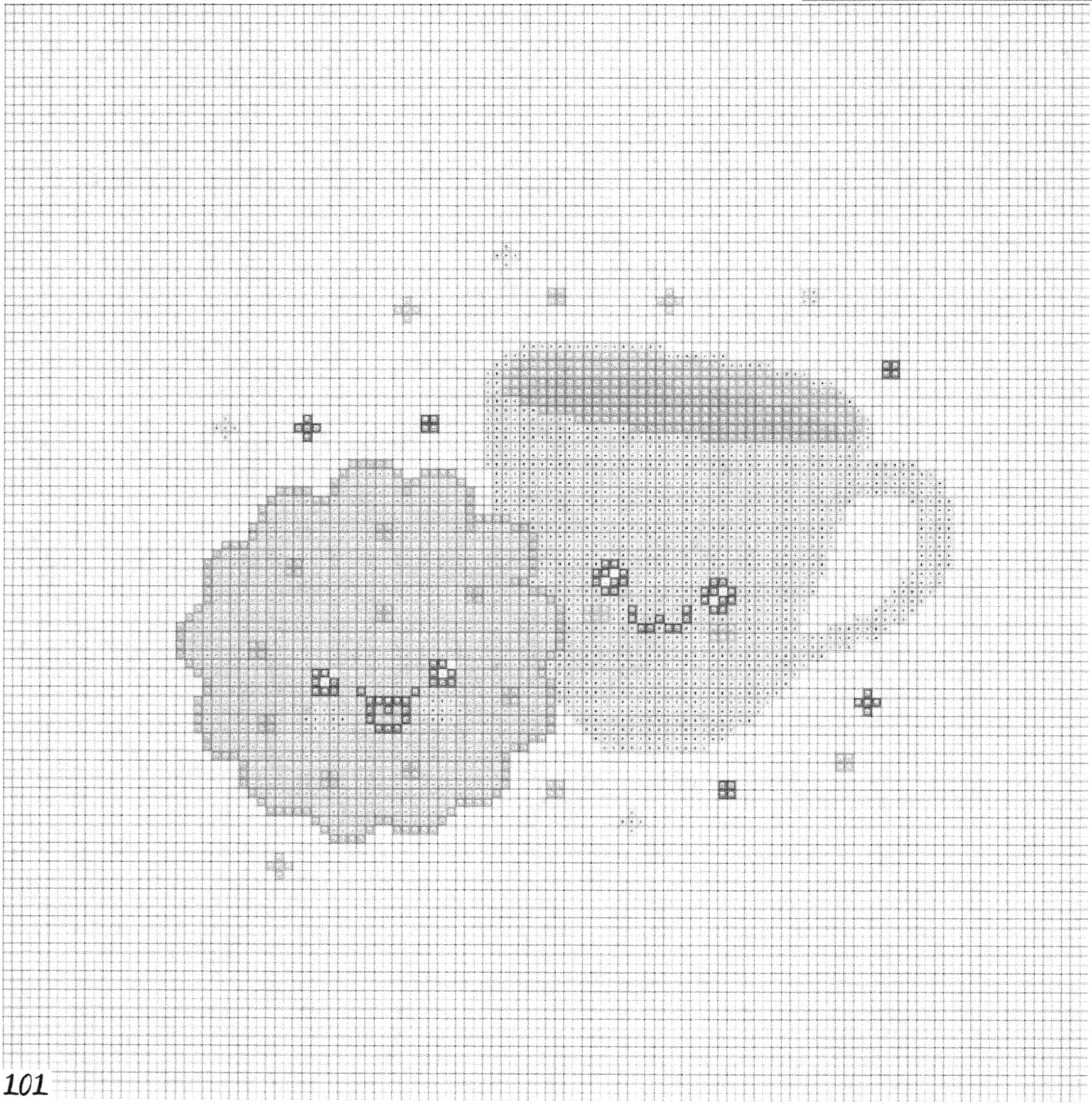

Strawberry milk

	Count	Code	Name
★	1153	3834	Grape Dark
▢	88	471	Avocado Grn V Lt
▲	468	899	Rose Medium
▤	837	3609	Plum Ultra Light
✛	737	3708	Melon Light
‿	2493	White	White

Matcha tea

		Count	Code	Name
★	■	107	327	Violet Dark
▢		219	703	Chartreuse
▲		298	907	Parrot Green Lt
⊞		28	3341	Apricot
⌘		652	224	Shell Pink Very Light
▤		894	225	Shell Pink Ult Vy Lt
✂		1521	3770	Tawny Vy Light
◡		440	White	White

Chips

		Count	Code	Name
★	■	1107	310	Black
□	▨	905	606	Orange-Red Bright
▲	▨	2895	444	Lemon Dark
+	▨	34	3706	Melon Medium
∪	☐	1579	White	White

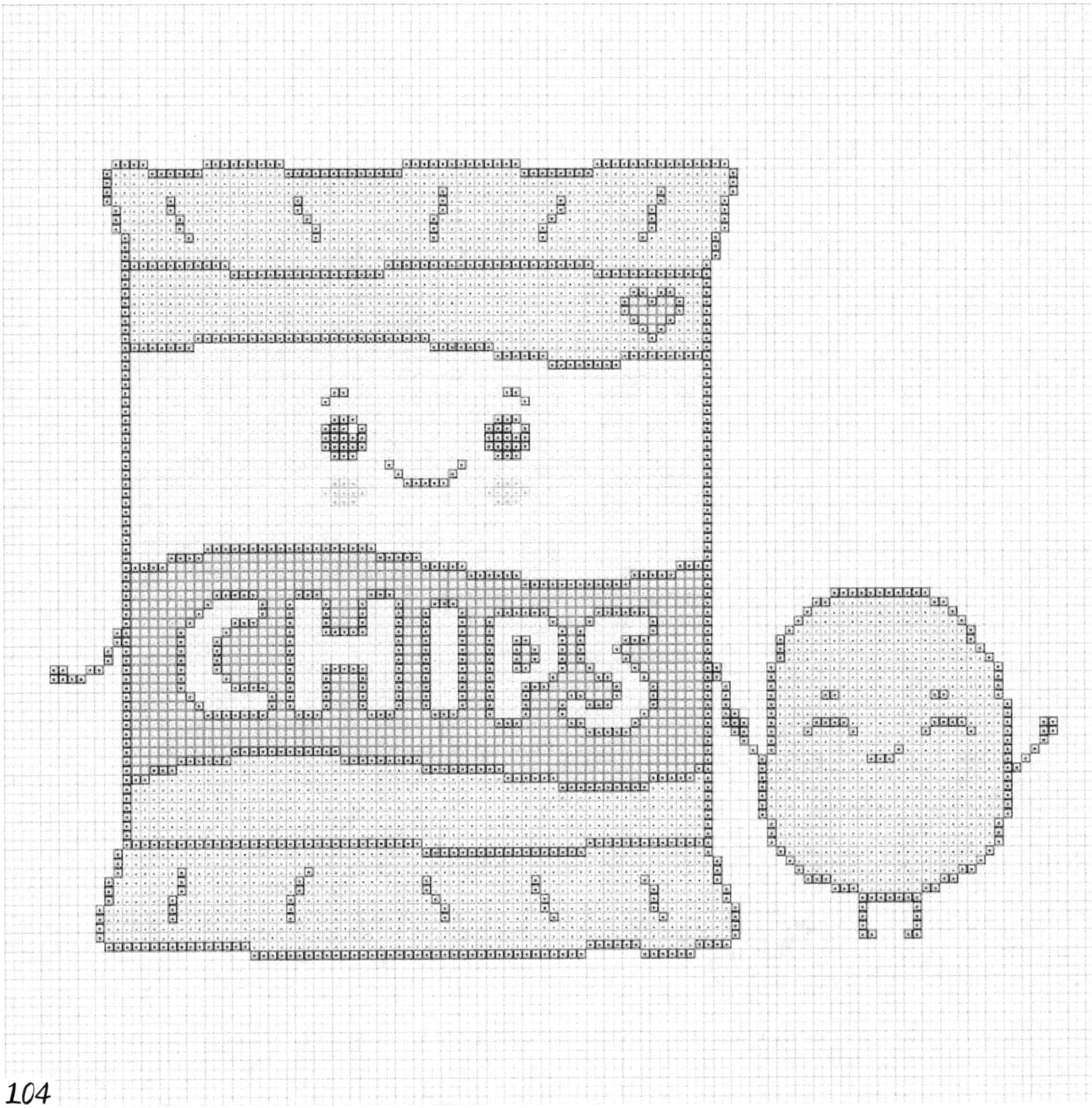